TEENS IN TWO WORLDS

TEENS IN TWO WORLDS

MIKE COPE

with Robert Oglesby, Jr.

Christian Communications
P.O. Box 150
Nashville, Tennessee 37202

Published by Christian Communications
A Division of Gospel Advocate Co.
P.O. Box 150, Nashville, TN 37202

ISBN 0-89225-347-9

Third Printing, July 1991

To Diane
A Beautiful Balance of Holiness
and Ministry

FOREWORD

The material in this book began coming together during my second year of preaching for the College Church in Searcy, Arkansas. While I met some university students who dreamed of ministering (as teachers, lawyers, secretaries, nurses, preachers, etc.) in the name of Jesus, there were many others whose dreams were clouded and misdirected by the world's quest for power, success and money.

We've spent lots of time in the church warning about the world's behavior—drugs, alcohol, sexual immorality, smoking and such. But the real battle with this world is at a much deeper level: the level of values. My fear is that we have let Hollywood, *People* and *Seventeen* magazines, and television advertisers mold us. Too often Christian teenagers develop an unhealthy attachment to the success symbols of this world.

The conflict over values and behavior should ultimately lead us back to Jesus. Many carry Christian assumptions because of their family without ever wrestling with the question, "Is Jesus 'the way, the truth, and the life'?" If he is, we must follow him—not because he will make us happy, wealthy, or fulfilled but because he is real. Having decided that Jesus is really the Lord, we will keep a holy distance from the world—just as he did. We will also plunge into the world with a message of hope—just as he came to bring hope.

The sermons I preached on "Christ and Culture" at the College Church were hammered into a manuscript that became the book and video series *Living in Two Worlds*. Now with lots of excellent help from Robert Oglesby, Jr. (thanks, Robert!), I hope the material can challenge Christian teenagers to be both in the world and separate from the world.

Mike Cope

CONTENTS

CHAPTER 1

The Third Race

The tension between a Christian and his society is highlighted in the story Tony Campolo relates of a child who entered his house, not knowing the preacher was visiting. Seeing his mom, the boy came running in holding a rat by the tail. With obvious excitement he choked out: "Look, Mom! Look at this rat I caught out behind the barn! I smashed its head in with a baseball bat! I threw rocks at it! I stomped on it! I spit on it and I, I, I . . ."

Then he looked up and saw the minister. Swallowing hard he said, "And, and, then the dear Lord called it home!"

This tension became obvious to me as I sat with some diving friends in a small cafe by the Atlantic Ocean one morning. We were waiting for breakfast since the weather had spoiled our planned excursion. Soon another group of scuba divers who knew my friends but not me joined us. One of them began describing the waitress in graphic (and disgusting) language. My buddies were dying inwardly—if only he knew I was a preacher!

Finally he paused long enough to ask, "What do you do?"

I calmly replied, "I preach for the Pine Valley Church."

He laughed hysterically and asked again, "Really, what do you do?"

I smiled and said, "I told you. I preach for the Pine Valley Church."

This time his smile was nervous as he glanced at one of my friends, who nodded in agreement. Quickly he straightened up, changed tones, and said, "My brother took a theology class at Duke." I was somewhat underwhelmed!

It is an awkward position we Christians are in. We are striving toward a spiritual world while we labor in an imperfect, sin-saturated world. How do we keep our eyes focused on Jesus when the world we live in rarely reflects Jesus?

What is the relationship between those who have been born again and the world where they were first born? What happens when Christ and our culture meet?

Christ and the Culture

The relationship between Christ and culture is not a new issue. Christians at the end of the second century struggled with it. The anonymous writer of "The Epistle of Diognetus" described the way we must be in the world but not of the world:

Yet while living in Greek and barbarian cities according as each obtained his lot and following the local customs both in clothing and in food and in the rest of life, Christians show forth a wonderful and confessedly strange character of the constitution of their own citizenship. They dwell in their own fatherlands but as if sojourners in them. They share all things as citizens and suffer all things as strangers. Every foreign country is their fatherland and every fatherland is their foreign country. They marry as all men. They bear children, but they don't expose their offspring. They offer free hospitality but guard their purity. Their lot is cast in the flesh but they do not live after the flesh. They pass their time upon the earth but they have their citizenship in heaven. They obey the appointed laws and they surpass the laws in their own lives.

Shortly after that was written, some Christians began calling themselves the Third Race. They weren't Jews, and they weren't exactly Gentiles. They struggled with the issue of relating to the world while holding citizenship in heaven.

The issue faced by those early Christians confronts us today. How do we relate to our world? Two key words from scripture help us answer that question.

The First Word: Holiness

Throughout the New Testament we read of saints. To some this conjures up images of superspiritual people— people who have hit all the good things in life, who have overcome all sins, who are ahead of everyone else. The Roman Catholic Church has influenced such thinking by putting certain individuals on a pedestal and calling them saints.

In the New Testament, however, saints are ordinary people in the church with flaws—not the spiritually elite, but all who have been called into Jesus Christ. We are a holy people, set aside by God for a special purpose (Titus 2:14). (For the Old Testament roots of this thought, see Deuteronomy 7:6, 14:2, and 26:18.)

God set us apart in baptism. He's declared us to be holy because of the atonement of Christ. Now we are called upon to live that way (1 Peter 1:15; James 1:27, 4:4). But how?

John (1 John 2:15-17) and Paul (2 Corinthians 6:14—7:1) emphasized the separation that should characterize Christians. Don't partake of the unholiness of the world, they warned us. Don't love the world by indulging in its values and evil practices.

Teenagers fight against their culture in this aspect because purity and holiness are usually not desirable characteristics. In fact, these qualities are looked down on by the teenage population as a whole. You often face ridicule by your peers if you aren't aware of the latest dirty joke, the worst scene in the R-rated movie, or street wise about the effects of certain drugs and alcohol. Christ calls us to be different. The question is, "How different should we be?"

We should purify ourselves from everything that contaminates body and spirit, perfecting holiness out of reverence for God (2 Corinthians 7:1). If we don't, the uniqueness that should permeate our lives will be absent.

The Second Word: Ministry

While our citizenship is in heaven, we are now residents

of this earth. We're pilgrims or aliens, but while we're here, we must live with and serve the people around us.

Consider the ministry of Jesus. He was here to serve (Mark 10:45), to help sinners (Mark 2:17), and he called on us to do the same thing. Our place is not in a monastery. We are to be out in the world, as Paul was, serving as ministers (1 Corinthians 9:19-23).

Both holiness and ministry are important. To be holy, our value system and actions must be different from those of the world. To minister we must be out in the world letting the influence of Christ be felt.

What happens if we have holiness but no ministry, or ministry but no holiness? What happens if we have both? Three models will help us answer those questions.

Spiritual Ostriches

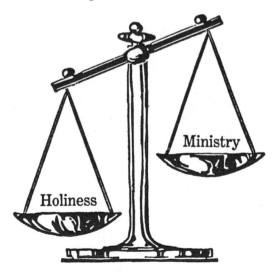

The first model is a radical separation from the world. These people would love to seclude themselves on a mountaintop far away from the temptation of sin. They like to completely surround themselves with other Christians, hoping they won't have to talk to a non-Christian all day long. There are a few moments of adventure into the sinful world before they scurry back to the safe hands of the community of believers.

Before the time of Jesus, some like-minded Jews separatists had gathered near the Dead Sea to protect their purity. Their famous scrolls (The Dead Sea Scrolls) have pointed toward their rejectionist outlook. The following is found in their "Scroll of the Rule": "And this is the rule for the members of the Community for those who volunteer to be converted from all evil and to cling to all the Teacher's commands according to his will; to separate themselves from the congregation of perverse men, to become a Community in the Law."

How many of us follow this example to a lesser degree? We like to be sheltered by having people around us who think as we do. We secretly desire to do business only with Christians, to be educated only with Christians, and to live only around Christians. We wind up as spiritual ostriches who bury our heads, choosing to ignore the lostness of the world. We require a controlled environment because our fragile condition can't stand the germs of our surroundings.

If that is our viewpoint, we are unbalanced rejectionists. We are hiding our light under a bushel. We may be proud of our light, but nobody sees it.

Chameleon Christians

The second model is the unbalanced Chameleon Christians. The chameleon lizard is known for being able to change colors to mix in with its surroundings. The animal is protected from harm by conforming to its environment. The Chameleon Christians are big on identifying with the world and "ministering" to its needs to the extent of losing their unique Christian lifestyle. It usually doesn't happen overnight, but it is just as dangerous. As Paul cautioned: "Do not conform any longer to the pattern of this world, but be transformed by the renewing of your mind" (Romans 12:2).

7

The lack of objection by many in Germany in the 1920s and '30s is an example of ungodly conformity. After Hitler came to power in 1933, it wasn't long until doctors, lawyers, ministers, theologians, and psychiatrists were working for the Nazis. It was a time that called for Christians to be radically different. You can't always flow with the cultural tide.

The second imbalance isn't light hidden under a bushel. It isn't light at all. There is only darkness. Chameleon Christians are socially infiltrating the world, but they are not spiritually distinct. Paul was saying in Philippians 2:14 and 15 that, "We are to shine like stars in the universe as we hold out the word of life." We are called to make a sharp contrast in this sinful world.

The Balanced Act

The third model is a balance of both holiness and ministry. It is the model Jesus left with his apostles and the balance that made the church a dynamic body that changed the world. It's a model that says that on one hand I must be holy; God calls me to distinctive living. But on the other hand, I must also have a life reaching out to the people who don't know Jesus. The church must be in the world without having too much of the world in the church.

Jesus spoke to this issue as he was about to leave his disciples (John 17:13ff). In his high priestly prayer he said, "Sanctify them, Father. Set them apart. Let them know they are not of the world. Yet, Father, I'm sending them into the world. They're ministers. They are to exercise a leavening influence in the world. They are salt and light. They are the aroma of good news" (paraphrased).

Our goal is to combine holiness and ministry—to be a light to a lost world. As a young boy, I remember going to Mammoth Cave in Kentucky. The guide led us to the very depths of the cave with various lights. We stopped on the trail, and our guide turned out the lights. I will never forget the feeling of utter darkness. My eyes were fully open, yet I couldn't see anything. After a few moments, my uncomfortableness turned into panic. Suddenly a single match was struck. My eyes immediately chased the tiny light in the vast darkness. My fears ceased, and my eyes welcomed the light. One match pushed back a whole cave filled with blackness. Our light must be distinct and available to a world filled with evil and darkness. If either holiness or ministry is missing from your life, then something is wrong with your view of Christ and culture.

The delicate balance we're seeking in this book of being in the world but not of the world is cleverly captured by John Fischer in this poem:

THE IN'S AND OUT'S OF IT
"In it, not of it," the statement was made
As Christian One faced the world, much afraid.
"In it, not of it," the call was made clear,
But Christian One got something stuck in his ear.
"Not in it, or of it" was the thing that he heard.
And knowing the world was painfully absurd,
He welcomed the safety of pious retreat,
And went to the potluck for something to eat

Now Christian Two, he knew what to do,
He'd show those fundies a thing or two!

How will the world ever give Christ a try
If we don't get in there and identify?
So, "In it, and of it," he said in his car,
As he pulled in and stopped at a popular bar.
"I'll tell them the truth as soon as I'm able
To get myself out from under this table."

Now along comes Christian Three jogging for Jesus,
In witnessing sweats made of four matching pieces.
His earphones are playing a hot Christian tune
About how the Lord is coming back soon.
"Not in it, but of it," he turns down the hill
And stops in for a bite at the Agape Grill.
Like the gold on the chain of his "God Loves You" bracelet,
He can have the world without having to face it.

While way up in heaven they lament these conditions
That come from changing a few prepositions.
"Not in it, or of it," Christian One thought.
But who in the world will know that he's not?
"In it, and of it," thought Christian Two.
But who in the world will know that he knew?
"Not in it, but of it," thought Christian Three.
But who in the world watches Christian TV?

And Jesus turns to Gabriel, shaking His head.
" 'In it, not of it,' wasn't that what I said?"[1]

---

[1]From John Fischer, *Real Christians Don't Dance* (Minneapolis: Bethany House Publishers, 1988) pp. 132-33. Used by permissio

THOUGHT QUESTIONS FOR CHAPTER 1

1. Is your church changing the world or is the world changing your church?
2. In which areas do you believe most Christians are more deficient: holiness or ministry?
3. How would a Bible personality like Daniel be treated if he was a teenager at your school? At your church? Why?
4. What would happen if all the Christians suddenly vanished from the face of the earth? What would the world be like in five years?
5. Which of these models best describes your youth group?
Spiritual Ostriches
Chameleon Christians
Balanced

CHAPTER 2

Success: The Fatal Attraction

Like a seductress, she can woo. As a magnetic field with a compass, she can pull irresistibly. Like the Sirens of ancient mythology, she can sing a sweet tune that compels you to sail to her isle. "She" is success: that golden goddess with the attractiveness of Aphrodite and the thunder of Poseidon.

We fall in love with her in school when we hear the high school cheer: "S-U-C-C-E-S-S. That's the way you spell success." Real food for thought! We pay homage to her around graduation when we select the boy and girl "Most Likely to Succeed."

And after graduating, we return to those schools periodically for the most sacred of worship assemblies to her—called reunions—times of judgment to reckon what we've done in this body, whether good or bad. Who cruised up in the BMW? Who pushed their battered Plymouth into the parking lot? Who married well? Who finished his Ph.D.? Who landed the most prestigious job?

Success is our national religion. We eat it, breathe it, caress it, baby it, worship it, and even worse, judge ourselves by it. If we think we've lived up to society's standards for success, we feel great about ourselves. If, on the other hand, we fall short, we feel like worthless zeros.

In America we tend to define success by the trinity of

wealth, power and fame. We bow down before them. If we cannot find them in life, we think we've missed our calling.

As God's people, have we managed to stay separate from society's view of success, or have we bought into that view?

Leonard Allen has written a piercing article that includes these words:

There's a growing tendency to adopt the narcissistic language of psychological self-help theories and masquerade it as gospel preaching. And, in the process, turn the gospel into a do-it-yourself formula for happy homes, robust sex, easy money and quick inner space. There's a trend toward allowing the "me" generation to dictate the terms in which we proclaim the gospel of the dying and rising Christ. In general, there's the powerful but subtle pressure to intertwine Christian values with middle class values, Christian destiny with American destiny, Christian sacrifice with the sacrifices of Republican economics, Christian success with Zig Ziglar's success. Only serious theological reflection, only fresh grappling with the biblical text in light of our past and present, can provide the resources for coping with the ferment and addressing the dangers.

If we judge ourselves on the basis of success, we need to carve our view of success from scripture. Two views of success appear in the parable of the rich man and Lazarus (Luke 16). The first is the high school reunion view (verses 19-21).

If you showed up at a reunion at Jerusalem High, how would you view the rich man? Based on the national trinity of wealth, power, and prestige, he's done well. The text says "he lives in luxury everyday." He's got a mansion in the best part of town. He's got purple robes and silk sheets. As he strolls up from his hand-carved, gold-trimmed chariot, people look at him and say, "There's a man who's made it in life!" When minutes are sent out later, they'll probably mention him first.

In contrast, we're embarrassed that somebody sent Lazarus an invitation. We try to forget he graduated from the same high school. He's covered with open sores. He stinks. We can hardly stand it as he walks in the door. He's malnourished, sitting at the rich man's gate and waiting for crumbs from his table.

But there's another view that comes from the parable—the eternal view. Lazarus died, and the angels carried him to Abraham's side. The rich man also died and was buried. And in Hades he looked up and saw Lazarus and wanted just a drop of water to cool his scorching tongue.

We've had a reversal of roles between the high school reunion and the eternal view of success. We're an eternal people if we're God's people. Let's consider three insights into success from the eternal view of this parable:

1. *Success has more to do with how you treat people than how they treat you.* The people at the Jerusalem reunion are glad the rich man came. They probably bow down to him. James noted how we have a tendency to treat the rich and famous better than we treat the poor and homely (James 2). Everyone wants the rich and famous at their party because it makes their event look successful.

By this view of success, Jesus did his best job, hit the highest point of his ministry, in the triumphal entry into Jerusalem (Luke 19). People ripped off their coats and cut down palm branches to put over the yellow brick road into the city.

But Luke told us that real success is found not on the road to Jerusalem, but on the cross just outside the city gates. Luke showed us that success is not how people treat you, but how you treat others. Jesus had been saying, "I've come for you. I've come to die." It was because he loved us so much that he allowed the soldiers to nail his hands to the cross.

If Jesus walked into a high school reunion, I think these are the kinds of questions he'd be asking: How have you been treating your friends lately? How about your enemies? What concern do you have for those with inadequate housing and nutrition?

2. *Success has more to do with God's view of you than with other people's view of you.* Again, if we start with the rich man at the high school reunion, he's doing quite well. He's probably in every "Who's Who" published—"Who's Who in Jerusalem," "Who's Who in Palestine," even the big

volume called "Who's Who in the Roman Empire." If success is how people view you, he has it made.

Sociologists tell us that we feel successful if the most successful people in our lives tell us we are successful. What makes children feel successful? When Mom and Dad tell them they're incredible kids. That's why I hate to hear parents jokingly refer to their kids as brats or messes. Once in awhile they may know by the tone of their voice that their parents are kidding, but when it's constant, they start to think of themselves that way.

Teenagers typically get their self-esteem from several different groups of people. One of the most important groups is their peers—the people around them at school or church, their immediate, "significant others." Teenagers want to be perceived as successful, especially by the opposite sex.

A girl wants to be asked out by the most popular boy in school, not necessarily because she wants to go out with *him,* but because she wants everybody to know she's going out with him. Her self-esteem depends on how others view her. A boy fantasizes about accomplishing great athletic feats to prove himself to that special someone in the stands. He wants to see himself as successful through the lenses of other people's glasses.

This dependency on other's perceptions of us leaves us desperate for their approval. One college girl came to my office sobbing about her immoral life of the previous semester which she had hoped would make her popular. A high school senior I knew was successful with youth groups because of his ability to give devotional talks on Sunday nights, and with his buddies at school because of his ability to guzzle a six-pack on Friday nights. The thread of consistency through his actions was the eagerness to gain his peers' approval.

If our view of success is to be correct, we can't seek success through other people's eyes. We need the significant other person in our lives to be God and to search for joy in his eyes.

1 Peter 2:4-10 is a good passage for helping teens build true, biblical self-esteem. Peter warns that we may often feel rejected by people around us. But that shouldn't be surprising since people also rejected Jesus. And just as he became the precious cornerstone of our faith, we are precious to God. Peter describes us as "a chosen people, a holy nation, a people belonging to God." That is true success!

3. *Success has to do more with internal qualities than with external circumstances.* It can't be right for millions of American women to feel like complete zeros because they can't measure up to the statistics of a twenty-year-old strutting on a ramp in Atlantic City. It can't be right to *heap honor* on a young man because of an athletic ability with

which he was born. We cannot, as God's people, buy into the concept of success through external circumstances.

Erma Bombeck once filled her humorous pen with serious ink and wrote the following words:

On the first Saturday of last month a 22-year-old U.S. tennis player hoisted a silver bowl over his head at center court at Wimbledon. On the day before five blind mountain climbers, one man with an artificial leg, an epileptic and two deaf adventurers stood atop the snow-capped summit of Mt. Ranier. It was a noisy victory for the tennis player who shared it with 14,000 fans, some of whom had slept on the sidewalks outside the club for six nights waiting for tickets. It was a quiet victory for the climbers who led their own cheering. There was a lot of rhetoric exchanged at Wimbledon regarding bad calls. At Mt. Ranier they learned to live with life's bad calls a long time ago . . . . In our search for heroes and heroines we often lose our perspective . . . . Hero is a term that should be awarded to those who, given a set of circumstances, react with courage, dignity, decency and compassion—people who make us feel better by having seen or touched them. I think the crowds went to the wrong summit and cheered the wrong champion.

God tells us he looks at the heart in 1 Samuel 16:7. He is not impressed with the external signs of success. God looks for faithfulness not successfulness. This concept should change the way you judge your success. I urge you to make God your significant other person so that your goal becomes to please him alone.

THOUGHT QUESTIONS FOR CHAPTER 2

1. What does society tell teens they must have to be successful?
2. Is it wrong to have one of the qualities in Question 1? Why, or why not?
3. What qualities does God look for in your heart?
4. How does a youth group judge its success or failure?

ACTIVITY

Put one student in a chair in the front of the class. Let students compliment the designated student on one of his or her internal qualities. This means no comments on their looks, dress or athletic ability. After a few minutes, choose someone else to sit in the chair.

A. The teacher can comment on the difficulty we have complimenting internal qualities.

B. Focus on how good it feels to have those great internal qualities identified by your peers.

CHAPTER 3

The Gospel According to Rambo

"Beads of sweat glisten. Pectoral muscles ripple. Veins bulge in steamy close-up. They call him a pure fighting machine—this glum-faced superhero with a Charles Atlas body. He's been sent on a mission to Viet Nam—a land that just a few years ago the nation was trying to forget. Improbably, or maybe all too probably, he has become America's newest pop hero. His name—Rambo."

So read *Time* magazine concerning Rambomania. Rambo is Sylvester Stallone's 1985 superhero. Many identify with him. He reflects not a way to change culture, but what culture already is. It's the *inborn* desire to control other people, to be powerful, to manipulate. It's J. R. Ewing with a machine gun.

Time also talked about Rambomania in the toy stores. You could buy a $150 replica of his high-powered bow and arrow, a Rambo knife, a Rambo automatic squirt gun, and Rambo vitamins. New Yorkers who wanted a raise from the boss could send a Rambo-gram.

This attitude influences our culture's talk about nuclear war. We complain that the Russians could kill everyone seven times while we could only do it four or five times. The emphasis is on power and control.

The German philosopher Friedrich Nietzsche said that the will to power is an innate desire. It's the desire to control other people. Nietzsche believed that God was dead—if he ever existed—and that man had to be in control. What Nietzsche's philosophy demonstrates is that if your greatest desire is to be powerful, you have to get rid of God, because God is bigger than you are.

These desires for Rambo-like power go back to the earliest days when the serpent said to Adam and Eve, "Would you like to be like God? Would you like to be powerful? Would you like to control? Would you like to see like God? To know like God? Then eat some of the fruit he's forbidden. He just doesn't want you to have the power he does." They wanted power as much as we do, so they ate the fruit.

Games People Play

Politicians play power games because they have positions of power. Sennacherib, Nebuchadnezzar, Alexander, Nero, and Hitler are names that drip with the sweat of power. They wanted more and more. Herod the Great even killed his sons rather than let them challenge his power. Solomon must also be added to the list. Samuel had warned the people of Israel, "You don't need a king, because he'll soak you for all you're worth. He'll crave power." And Solomon did. He enslaved and overtaxed his people.

Not all politicians are like this. Some want to change society for good. But others got where they are because they like power. They drink it up.

An American Life—One Man's Way to Watergate is Jeb Stuart MacGruder's story of his involvement in Watergate. MacGruder was a young, articulate, well-educated Californian who was called to take on a responsible position within the administration of President Richard Nixon. MacGruder details how he forgot his ethics, violated his morality, and put behind him all he'd learned about right and wrong. Why? "I was close to the seat of power," he explained.

Near the end of his autobiography, MacGruder wrote, "For fifteen years I fought to reach the pinnacle of our society. I got very close to the top and I found that it wasn't all it was supposed to be. To get there and stay there you have to pay a price too high in your private life. Obviously, in my case, ambitions led to disaster." MacGruder got caught. Many others don't.

Power games occur in dating. One good example is withholding love. It's the Principle of Least Interest. Never make an emotional commitment, never tell your date that you enjoy the relationship, and you can exercise control. For example, a couple has been dating for a year, but he's never told her he's glad they're dating. He never says anything about their relationship. He just keeps asking her out, and she's not sure why. He's emotionally aloof because if he's aloof, he's in control. Although he thinks he's smart, he's probably just watched too many old James Bond movies where he learned to be emotionally detached while romantically involved.

Another game in dating is withholding forgiveness. You may learn something of a person's past, or that person may offend you. But you never forgive the person, so your knowledge of his or her past becomes your trump card. Whenever there's friction in the relationship, you bring it up. It's a power game that says, "I have control over you. I'm the offended party. So let me have my way now."

These games are played in marriages, too. Husbands withhold love. Some never tell their wives they love them. They just come home to eat at the end of the day. The wife is left wondering, *Am I still attractive to him? Is our marriage going anywhere?* He's playing a power game.

A husband can also play power games by misusing his leadership and handing down decisions without thinking of his wife's needs. He knows the Bible passages about being the head of the family, but not the ones about loving his wife.

Another power game is played when husbands compliment other women. "Doesn't Alice always have her house in order?" But his wife knows he means, "Why do I have to live in a pig sty?" Or he says, "Have you ever noticed how

Suzie keeps fit?" The real message is, "Why don't you carve some fat off your hips?" She gets these subtle messages. When he tells her something about these other women, he's got power over her. She's left worried and wondering where she stands.

Wives play power games, too. Those who have bought into the radical element of the women's movement have been encouraged to face bossy husbands by being bossy wives.

Teenagers also play power games. They threaten Mom and Dad with, "If you don't let me have my way, I'll pack up and leave," or "I'm going to do something horrible that you'll always regret." A young lady at Robert's church was playing this power game when she wrote the following poem.

> She bowed her head as if to pray.
> She knew in her heart this would be the last day;
> The last day for anger, suffering, or pain,
> The last day to cry or to see a soft rain,
> The last day for responsibilities, worries or doubts,
> The last day to know what this world's all about.
> Good-bye everyone.
> It's over at last,
> And she was gone
> In one short blast.

She never intended to put a gun to her head, but she conveniently left the poem where her parents would find it, and she hoped it would scare them into saying yes to her demands.

Employers play power games. They do it by causing their employees to worry about losing their jobs. They never express appreciation. A boss may say, "I've just got to cut back on the staff one of these days."

Of course, employees play power games, too. They may

say, "If you try to make me do anything I don't want to do, I'll file a grievance with the union." While there are legitimate places for unions, Christians shouldn't use them as a way to manipulate others.

Religious legalists could be described as people who want to work their way into heaven by Christian deeds. This group knows how to play power games, too. They can't stand the thought of being saved by someone else—even God. They enjoy the thought of saving themselves by their numerous acts of service. A legalist envisions God's taking up the last few items he couldn't quite make. (Grace is not God taking up the slack; it is God taking over.)

In friendship some play power games as well. In his book *The Friendship Factor*, Alan Loy McGinnis talked about three kinds of manipulators in friendships. First, there are the "take charge" manipulators. They always have to call the shots. You always go to *their* restaurants. You always do what *they* want to do. They aren't happy unless they're in the driver's seat.

Second, there are the "poor me" manipulators. "Poor me. Things are so bad. You don't know how bad they are. The things last week have been solved, but I've got worse things this week." I counseled a lady like that one time. Nothing could make her happier than a tragedy that gave her an excuse to "poor me" you.

Third is the "need to be needed" type. This person says, "I'm always available. You can always tell me." It may be a mother who wants a daughter to have marital problems and come running with "Oh, Mom, I've got problems." Such a mother loves to be needed.

Jesus' Power

If anyone could have played power games, it was Jesus. He was "in the very nature of God" (Philippians 2:6). Before he came to earth, Jesus was equal with God. He was God himself, God the Son. That's an impressive portfolio for power. He was in the nature of God, yet he didn't consider equality with God something to be grasped. He came to a culture that thrived on power, and he chose powerlessness. He chose the way of love rather than the way of Rambo. He chose love over power. He "made himself nothing" (Philippians 2:7).

Jesus didn't come as a Superbaby or Superboy who dazzled his friends with magic. Some people have wished he had. There are some early nonbiblical "gospels" composed in the second and third centuries. One says that Jesus killed some of his friends when they made him mad. Another says he was playing with a little boy who fell off a roof, and Jesus went down and raised him from the dead. A third tells of his making a little clay bird and bringing it to life.

These stories are not in harmony with the biblical account. The Bible says that Jesus was born as a vulnerable infant to parents who were known to few people in a tiny town in an insignificant province: "Taking the very nature of a servant, being made in human likeness" (Philippians 2:7).

During his manhood, people tried to force him to play power games. In Luke 4:9-11 Satan was saying, "Climb to the top of the temple, jump off, and let tens of thousands of angels come to your rescue." That was a call to play power games. Jesus wanted people to repent, leave everything, and follow him. Those were high demands for discipleship, and many would turn him down. Satan was saying, "If you jump off the temple, people will flock to you." But Jesus wouldn't play his game.

On another occasion, 5,000 men gathered in the desert and tried to make him king by force. They needed a military general to lead them into Jerusalem to oust the Romans. Jesus wouldn't play that game either.

In the Garden of Gethsemane, Peter tried to play the game. When Judas came with the authorities, Peter whipped out his sword and cut off Malchus's ear. But Jesus said, "Peter, I'm not playing that game."

Remember the power games of James and John? They came to Jesus and said, "Master, can we have the places of power when you come into your kingdom?"

Jesus replied, "Let me talk to you about suffering."

Jesus steadfastly refused to play power games. He took the nature of a servant. He refused to manipulate people. He chose love over power. "And being found in appearance as a man, he humbled himself and became obedient to death—even death on a cross!" (Philippians 2:8). Jesus was not a Rambo storming the gates of Jerusalem with his automatic weapon. He was a broken man, crucified shamefully on a Roman cross outside the city gates. He chose love, even in the form of suffering, over power games.

Learning the Lesson of Jesus

How does all of this apply to us? First, we must realize that God possesses ultimate power. Any power we have has been given to us by a higher authority. Our problem comes when we begin to think we created the power, or when we use power for our own selfish desires. God can't use you in a powerful way until you rely on his power instead of your own. Paul was willing to lose everything so that he could know Christ and the power of his resurrection (Philippians 3).

In his second letter to the church at Corinth, Paul put it another way: "To keep me from becoming conceited because of these surpassingly great revelations, there was given me a thorn in my flesh, a messenger of Satan, to torment me. Three times I pleaded with the Lord to take it away from me. But he said to me, 'My grace is sufficient for you, for my power is made perfect in weakness.' Therefore I will boast all the more gladly about my weaknesses, so that Christ's power may rest on me" (2 Corinthians 12:7-9).

That's power in weakness. It's the way of the cross. Rely on your weakness. God will use you more in weakness when you count on his grace than when you're trying to stand on your own power. Several years ago, Wally Wilkerson was diagnosed as having multiple sclerosis. He had to quit his job as a youth minister, and many prayed that the Lord would take away the disease. We couldn't understand why a faithful servant of God would be hampered by this disability. It was not long before Wally provided the answer. He was able to share Jesus daily with large numbers of non-Christian people with M.S. His ministry was stopped at first glance, but the Lord has opened a new ministry even through Wally's weakness. He now reaches more non-Christians every day than he did as a full-time minister.

Second, we should learn to value meekness. Meekness is not a big word in the Rambo vocabulary. It sounds "wimpy." But meekness means you have your strength under control. There's still power, but it submits to love. Instead of living with love for power, we live, as Huey Lewis sings, by "the power of love." They are entirely different things.

Some Christians in Philippi were apparently playing power games. They were jockeying for position. Paul was telling them, "Your attitude should be the same as that of Christ Jesus." He didn't talk about Jesus just out of biographical interest. He wanted the Christians there to live that way. Instead of struggling for power in the Philippian church, they were to give in to the power of love.

If we're going to live with a connection between Christ and culture, we must oppose power plays. We must oppose efforts to use people, control them, manipulate them. We must live by the power of the cross.

Power games will ruin the people you play with, and they'll ruin you, too. If you've been manipulating people and controlling them against their will, go back to the groundwork of Philippians 2 and start living a life of service.

THOUGHT QUESTIONS FOR CHAPTER 3

1. The chapter names several power games that are commonly played. What other examples could you give?

2. Is it harder to have power and control it or not have power and envy those who have power?

3. What situations did Jesus choose to show his love rather than his power? (John 3:1-17) (Mark 15:21-41)

4. How do you feel when someone uses his power to control you?

5. Does love or power motivate you to obey God?

CHAPTER 4

Sex: Dr. Ruth vs. Bible Truth

Imagine that suddenly some kind of volcanic eruption buried the United States. Even the Rockies were encased. About two centuries from now, archaeologists dig down to where our civilization was. What would they find? What would they say about us?

They might say that we were fascinated with success, that we were power hungry, that we were materialistic. And what if they found some magazines that weren't completely ruined by lava or some tapes of television advertising or newspaper ads? Wouldn't they find that the key to selling was sex? They'd see sex used to sell perfume, blue jeans, aftershave lotion, ballpoint pens, fertilizer—anything you can think of.

They might find the Michigan State study that showed that soap operas average two sexual acts per program—94 percent between couples who aren't married. They would logically conclude that we were a sex-oriented society.

In his book *Christians in the Wake of the Sexual Revolution*, Randy Alcorn tells of two days he spent watching television:

> Because I don't watch much television, I wanted to get a broad and accurate exposure to current programming. So I bought an issue of *TV Guide* and spent two vacation days flipping from

channel to channel, watching m̲ never seen (and, Lord willing, I will never see

I saw several unmarried couples ▹vered an X-rated bakery in New York and ¿ in New Jersey, listened to a sex researcher ¢ ⁊w, and watched one movie in which everyon₍ ₊ed and another of a brutal rape in a New Engl̲ ₌ usual corruption and adultery on "Dynasty' ₌ering game show host making sexual comment and X-rated story lines with B-rated acting on

Alcorn was describing what people would find if they unearthed our civilization and watched the programs that come into our homes all day and evening.

What if they listened to our music? I'm sure they would find the raunchy, sexual lyrics in some rock music nearly as bad as those of some Country-Western music, and that's pretty bad. They might hear songs like this one from George Michael:

> I swear I won't tease you.
> Won't tell you no lies.
> I don't need no Bible.
> Just look in my eyes.
> I've waited so long, Baby.
> Now we're friends.
> Every man's got his patience,
> And here's where mine ends.
> I want your sex. . . . .

Now MTV allows these musical heroes to get their message across visually, just in case you didn't understand the words.

What if they came across our pornography? They might be shocked if they began flipping through *Playboy*, but they could find some other publications that make *Playboy* look tame. The U.S. Commission on Pornography took a random survey and found that one in five males and one in ten females had their first exposure to pornography by age twelve.

They might find movies that were popular in the 1980's, like "Dirty Dancing," or "Casual Sex." The interesting thing is that so many teenagers see these movies. And they don't see them just once: they pay good money to watch them over and over.

The archaeologists of the future would probably conclude that we spend one-third of our time having sex, one-third planning to have sex, and the other third talking about having sex.

It is obviously a major part of the teenager's world. In 1986, the *Chicago Tribune* surveyed 2300 teenagers from 58 foreign countries. They asked each teen to list the top three issues in his/her life. They also put 305 American teenagers through the very same survey. The 2300 foreign teenagers didn't put sex in their top three issues. However, 304 of the 305 American kids listed sex in their top three issues.

I believe there are some reasons why sex is a major issue. Kathleen Fury researched some changes in our society. Her study revealed some drastic changes in the puberty timetable and age kids marry. Compare the years of 1870 and 1987:

Menstruation	Age of First Menstruation	Age of Marriage
1870	16.5	18
1987	12	22.8

In 1870, there was a short time between physical maturity and sex within a marriage relationship. In 1987, there is a 10-year span of sexual tension. This makes it difficult to remain pure, and many young people lower their standards because it seems impossible. The good news is that you can stay sexually pure, but you will have to work harder at it than your parents did.

Another factor is that early dating leads to early sex. Brent Miller and Terrence Olsen surveyed 2400 teens, and found that the younger a girl begins to date, the more likely she is to have sex before graduating from high school. The chart below gives statistics from this survey.

Age of Dating	Percent Who Have Sex Before Graduation
12 years	91%
13 years	56%
14 years	53%
15 years	40%
16 years	20%

Most of you probably think your parents are too strict, but after looking at this chart, when would you want your kids to begin dating?

We need to look for truth in our sexual decisions. The television is filled with people like Dr. Ruth, who give advice, but who don't use God's plan for a basis. Let's consider four basic principles:

1. God created sex. The media in the world would like for you to think sex was their invention, but God was the one who created this great idea. He could have made us all one gender. He could have come up with another way for the race to continue, but he made male and female (Genesis 1:27). No one should have to apologize for having sexual feelings or thoughts, because God made us sexual beings. If we want to find out about a product, we ask the inventor. If we want to know about sex, we need to examine God's Word for our information.

2. Sex was created for married people. Most teens will never hear how beautiful sex is from a church pulpit or a classroom teacher. Sex is usually not really discussed within our church walls. It has become a subject you talk about in other places, but not in a church building.

Do you remember watching your mom place your Christmas present under the tree? The worst part was that you couldn't open it until Christmas morning. The anticipation kept you from sleeping the night before because you were so excited.

Sex is a gift from God to people who will commit to a married relationship. "For this reason a man will leave his father and mother and be united to his wife, and they will become one flesh" (Genesis 2:24). Some teens are like a young baby playing around the Christmas gifts. The baby unwraps the present because of immaturity. The baby sees the pretty paper, and he proceeds to rip open the gift. The problem is some people treat sex in much the same way. They don't want to wait, so their immaturity causes them to open the gift too early. The problem is they build up no anticipation because they didn't wait. The other problem is they will find that opening the gift again will not be as special the next time.

There is a whole book in the Old Testament that describes how great sex is between a husband and wife. If you ever study the Song of Solomon in Bible class, the teacher might begin mumbling parts or skipping sections. Don't let him! It describes how good sex is in a committed relationship. It is discussed in the New Testament, also. Paul wrote:

The husband should fulfill his marital duty (speaking about the sexual relationship) to his wife, and likewise the wife to her husband. The wife's body does not belong to her alone but also to her husband. In the same way, the husband's body does not belong to him alone but also to his wife. Do not deprive each other except by mutual consent and for a time, so that you may devote yourselves to prayer. Then come together again so that Satan will not tempt you because of your lack of self-control (1 Corinthians 7:3-5).

The act of sex is not meant to be selfish pleasure. It is an act of giving your mate physical and emotional pleasure. God gave us sex, and he tells us what is the most beneficial teaching for that relationship.

3. Sexual intercourse was not created for those outside of marriage. Sex can be a very wonderful thing, but man can corrupt many good things. A knife can be placed in a surgeon's hand, and he can save someone's life. Someone can take that same knife and take a person's life away. Sexuality is the same way. Within its God-given boundaries, it is beautiful. But if we abuse it, it can be very harmful.

God's people are called to a holy lifestyle (1 Thessalonians 4:3-8; Ephesians 5:3-7; 1 Corinthians 6:12-20). Two words are used in the New Testament for the violation of this holiness—fornication and adultery. Fornication means intimate sexual relationship outside of marriage. It could be homosexuality, adultery, or premarital sex. Adultery is more specific. It means sex in which one of the partners is married to another person.

Why should we be sexually pure? Let me give you two reasons: First, God says to. That may be the easiest answer. If you've just bought a computer and you ask the people you bought it from, "Why can't I wash the insides with soap and water?" the best answer might be that the manufacturer warns against it. The company made the computer. Its engineers know what's inside and what's harmful to it. Likewise, God made sex, and he set boundaries so we wouldn't abuse it. He knows us. He made us. He knows what will happen if we abuse our sexuality.

A youth minister in Texas told of a junior high girl who went on a church retreat. Her lifeless eyes showed sadness that was so out of place in a room full of laughter. Her physical beauty guaranteed popularity in any school, but her spirit contained a different message. Her life had been joyful, but she could hardly remember what that feeling was like anymore. She was 14 years old, and he was a 17-year-old jock. When they began dating, she became somebody. She enjoyed the new attention that came through their relationship, but the relationship had gradually become more and more physical. One night he told her he wanted her to go all the way, or he would walk away. She gave in to his demands, and he left her a few months later. How long would she carry the scars? She had gone eight months without joy, and the scars still showed.

God never wanted you to experience the pain that young lady felt. He knows how long it takes for the scars to heal, and he knows some of the scars may never heal. God wants you to feel real love, but you must obey his instructions for your sexual standards.

Second, sex was intended for a complete commitment. All of us who counsel find people whose lives are messed up because they experimented beyond God's boundaries. They thought that being unfaithful sexually wouldn't affect other aspects of their lives. That's wrong. Sex is part of a full union. In marriage it's part of a lot of different unions—of spirits, of commitments, of time together. You can't separate it and say, "We're going to have this sexual relationship and forget about the other relationships." The beauty of marriage is that God's people say, "I'm taking you until death separates us." Sex blossoms on this secure basis. We all love having that security in a committed relationship, so don't let someone talk you into sex without the real commitment of marriage.

Having asked why we should be pure, we can now ask, how can we remain pure? First, avoid sexually dangerous or tempting situations. Empty houses and lonely roads are bad places to go on a date. Most sexual activity between teenagers occurs between 3:00 and 5:00 p.m. in one of their homes. The problem we are dealing with is accountability. As a minister, I don't put myself in situations that don't keep me accountable to someone.

Psychologist Henry Brandt's son was upset because his father wouldn't let him go out alone on a date in a car. "What's wrong, Dad?" he asked. "Don't you trust me?"

His dad said, "In a car? Alone at night with a girl? I wouldn't trust me. Why should I trust you?"

Second, don't let your physical urges rule your relation-ship. Kids are always asking, how far is too far? I don't have any clear-cut answers, but I do have some strong opinions. Most of the questions are concerning petting. This is simply the touching of sexual organs, just short of sexual intercourse.

I see one major problem with petting. It only stimulates. It never satisfies. Petting encourages you to go farther sexually. I have a hard time reading 1 Corinthians 6:18 and condoning petting. The word used in this passage is "flee." To me it means to run quickly. The story that comes to mind is Potiphar's wife trying to seduce Joseph. He didn't think about it. He ran so fast his cloak came off. Now that is how you flee sexual immorality. My question is, "Is petting on a date fleeing from sexual immorality?" Can you defend it as an appropriate action for a disciple of Jesus?

Third, don't feed your mind sexual material. We are ruled by our thoughts, and our thoughts are ruled by what we feed our minds. We can't feed our minds pornography and sexually explicit videos without it affecting us. In talking to young people I've found those movies seem to flash back in their minds. The scenes they watched in the movie are sometimes replayed on their date. Read Philippians 4, and start feeding on the good things.

And finally, remember who is in you. 1 Corinthians 6:18-20 tells us we carry the Holy Spirit. In our struggle between the flesh and the Spirit, we face a battle similar to the one Jesus was involved in with the money changers at the temple. One of them had to go. Jesus pushed out the money changers, but will you let him win the battle in your heart to stay pure?

4. Sexual sins can be forgiven and overcome. The Bible doesn't say that sexual sins are unforgiveable. Jesus met several immoral people. The woman caught in adultery, the

woman at Jacob's well—he saw what these women could be. He treated them with a gentleness that we should imitate.

If you become involved in sexual sin, I would suggest you try the following steps.

A. Tell a trusted mature adult about your problem. You should become accountable to him/her as you work through the problem.

B. Stop putting yourself in situations where you will be alone with a person of the opposite sex. Begin group dating with your friends. You won't have a problem with sexual temptation if there are 15 people crammed into the back seat of your car.

C. Pray for help from the spiritual forces of God.

D. If you can't stop after taking these steps. You need to break off the relationship. I know this seems cruel, but God calls us to love him first and foremost. Anything that interferes with that relationship should be let go.

THOUGHT QUESTIONS FOR CHAPTER 4

1. Why did God command that sex should be inside of the marriage relationship?

2. What bad things might occur if you could have sex with anybody whenever you wanted?

3. Why is purity not admired by our culture?

4. Read 1 Thessalonians 4:1-8, discover at least three reasons we ought to be pure.

5. Why is sexual immorality a devastating sin? (Read 1 Corinthians 6:12-20.)

CHAPTER 5

"The Gospel According to Alex P. Keaton"

The first, most obvious, criterion for success in our society is money, or at least the appearance of money. We're very aware of exclusive neighborhoods, right cars, exotic vacations, designer clothing, expensive watches, etc., because these are evidence of doing well.

I recently spent some time with a man who meets all the monetary requirements for success. Things are going his way financially—a must in the roaring '80s. He understands the *quality* that is available to those who can afford it, true unlimited consumption, that leaves no doubts of whether someone has succeeded or not.

The man's portfolio, while not too diversified, is heavy with commodities. He understands investment and security, an imperative since the crash of October, '87. Though he's not a broker, he could stay with the best in the market. Shearson-Lehman-Hutton would be glad to have him.

And to make him the perfect representative of the Yuppie generation, he's a bit greedy. No quality is more denounced or more secretly admired in America than covetousness.

I appreciate the honesty of the 1987 hit movie "Wall Street." Michael Douglas plays Gordon Gekko, a powerful, money-thirsty corporate raider. In one scene he pleads with the stockholders of Teldar Paper Corporation to accept his takeover bid:

Greed is good. Greed is right. Greed works. Greed clarifies, cuts through and captures the essence of the evolutionary spirit. Greed—in all of its forms—greed for life, for money, for love, knowledge, has marked the upward surge of mankind and greed, you mark my words, will not only save Teldar Paper but that other malfunctioning corporation called the USA.

The man I've been with would love Donald Trump, a real hero for the 80's and 90's. About a year ago Trump bought a private yacht for $29 million. Of course it took around $8 million to fix it up a bit.

The yacht has eleven double guest suites, each complete with stereo, CD, VCR, and color TV. It has a cinema with seating for eighteen, a small waterfall, a huge barbecue deck, a disco with flashing lights, 210 phone lines, three elevators, a solid gold sink, and an infirmary with better equipment than many hospitals.

When asked why he bought the yacht since he doesn't care much for boats and won't have time for it, Trump replied: "quality means everything." He wanted not a boat but the best boat in the universe.

The spirit of materialism showed up in a 1988 survey of Baby Boomers in *Rolling Stone Magazine*. In two articles called "Portrait of a Generation," those around 20-40 were asked to compare their generation to that of their parents. When asked which emphasized being involved in church more, 8 percent said their own, while 75 percent said their parents' generation. But when asked about being success-oriented and getting ahead in business, 66 percent thought it applied more to their generation, while only 16 percent said it described their parents'.

If the tide of materialism is turning, it didn't show up in a survey given by UCLA's Higher Education Research Institute to 1988 incoming college freshmen. The study revealed that the "greed factor" with these 300,000 students was higher than ever in the twenty-two years of testing.

The nice thing for us about this spirit is that it goes nicely with Christianity—at least a certain version of Christianity. Of course you have to overlook a few verses, like . . .

"Any of you who does not give up everything he has cannot be my disciple . . ." (Luke 14:33).

"Blessed are you who are poor, for yours is the kingdom of God. . . . But woe to you who are rich, for you have already received your comfort . . ." (Luke 6:20, 24).

"How hard it is for the rich to enter the kingdom of God! Indeed, it is easier for a camel to go through the eye of a needle than for a rich man to enter the kingdom of God" (Luke 18:25).

"Foxes have holes and birds of the air have nests, but the Son of Man has no place to lay his head" (Luke 9:58).

"You still lack one thing. Sell everything you have and give to the poor, and you will have treasure in heaven. Then come, follow me" (Luke 18:22).

"Watch out! Be on your guard against all kinds of greed; a man's life does not consist in the abundance of his possessions" (Luke 12:15).

But who wants to be picky when you're trying to prove something? By baptizing the secular language of Wall Street, we have the health and wealth gospel.

The man I've been with recently is an appropriate

representative for the past decade. If he were in ministry, we'd probably call him a success.

Actually I've only been with him in my office with my Bible opened to Luke 12. This man we'd be tempted to call a success was called by Jesus a fool. He had made the mistake of putting his crops in his heart, thinking life was found in the abundance of things.

Materialism is the spirit of our age—both in and out of God's church. You see it in descriptions of people. When someone asks, "How much is he worth?" usually the answer is not, "More than the whole world because he's made in the image of God," but rather, "Around 2.5 million dollars." You see it in career decisions made on the basis of financial figures rather than where God wants us to be. You see it in patterns of voting. There's a movement toward conservatism in the United States, not because people are more conservative on specific issues, but because they have more possessions to conserve.

The Great Divider

Money is also the great divider in our communities, relationships and churches. Money determines the neighborhood in which you will live. It determines which school you may attend. It determines whether or not you will go to college. It decides whether you will get a brand new car for graduation or a previously owned car that barely runs. It dictates whether you will be a member of an exclusive country club or not. It may determine who you date because you may not be comfortable with someone who has much more or quite a bit less than you do. It may even determine which church you attend. Some people feel they don't fit in some churches if they aren't at least middle class. If they can't pay for all the youth activities or buy the latest fashions, they fear rejection from that congregation. This goes against everything that Jesus tried to teach. The poor and oppressed should be treated with honor and respect. We are individuals, yet Jesus calls us to be unified in spirit. The Lord hates division among his people whatever the reason.

Money is an evil force when it separates us from being open to relationships with all groups of people! There are churches that will not reach out to people who are living close to their building because of their economic level. When that happens, God cringes at our insensitivity. He didn't tell us to preach only to the rich and famous or the white and middle class. Greed is a dangerous side effect of money, but separation from people is just as dangerous.

The God of Success

Many churches today make claims that God didn't promise. They promise health and wealth for all those in God's tender care. They don't call you to sacrifice. They want you to invest in God.

Reverend Ike proclaimed his cultural message wrapped in the gospel by saying:

God doesn't want anyone to be poor. If you believe in him, you will believe in yourself. And, if you believe in yourself, you will get rich. I'm rich and that's because I believe in God and I believe in Reverend Ike.

The only problem is, what about our brothers and sisters in Western Kenya today? Many of them scrape to get by.

They suffer starvation from famine just like everyone else over there. What about the brothers and sisters behind the Iron Curtain whose financial position often goes down as their faithfulness to Christ goes up?

Jay Kesler's insights are right on target:

I'm amazed how many young people will not look at a car that is not at least BMW quality. They want quality food, quality watches, quality homes, quality enjoyment, quality everything—the best that materialism can buy. . . . If anyone should be able to see through and reject the materialistic philosophy, it should be the Christian church. But I fear we've so adapted ourselves to the cultural norm that we're not in a strong position to lead our youth to a more biblical standard. The church is far quicker to applaud and embrace the "conservative" self-centered values prevalent among youth today than it was to accept the justice-seeking, other-centered idealism of young people in the sixties.

An article in a religious magazine listed twenty-five reasons you might offer someone who's on the verge of becoming a Christian. They included: the most practical way to live, the way to realize success, the best investment of time and money, the way to help your country continue to be Christian, the way to preserve freedom in the USA, a cure for worry, the way to obtain better health and longer life, the way to enjoy financial advantages.

I'd hate to tell somebody to become a Christian for those reasons. What if he knew something about the life of Jesus? He might say, "Well, maybe Jesus wasn't a follower of God, because he wasn't wealthy." What if he knew about Paul? He could turn nearly any place in Second Corinthians and read, "I know what it's like to be without." And what if he knew about the people to whom Hebrews was written? Their property had been plundered because they chose to follow Jesus.

As Carl Henry has said, "The current philosophy 'Be born again and God will put you in clover,' needs divine editing to read, 'Get right with God and he will show you how many excesses you can do without.' "

We must teach against the health and wealth philosophy before a new generation comes up within our churches singing this version of *Jesus Loves Me*.

> Jesus loves me, this I see,
> For He gives me cars for free.
> Little minks to me belong.
> I am rich and it ain't wrong.
> —O'Shea

49

We need to develop a system of priorities not built on wealth. Let's look at one family who didn't buy "the American dream." This family is satisfied to live on a modest income in a modest house. The husband passed up several opportunities for job advancement with pay increases because he's happy where he is. They don't have the nicest cars in town. They don't take extravagant vacations. Their kids don't have new stereo equipment, but they all seem happy.

They live a relatively simple life, and they're not judgmental of those who live better. They're content to be where they are. People who know them feel sorry for them They think, "Old Bob could have done better for himself." The in-laws think, "If he'd take some of those jobs, they could live in the best part of town. He could be moving up. No telling where he might be in five years." People think he's ridiculous for the decisions he's made, but he and his family are happy.

This husband passed up many material rewards in order to maintain the important things in life. He used a different priority system than the world's. A great example of this principle is found in the story of Lot (Genesis 13). He and Abram had to part directions, and Lot was given a choice. He saw land that held earthly riches, but Lot didn't think about the spiritual consequences. He pitched his tent in the fertile plains around the city of Sodom. His pursuit of wealth nearly brought destruction upon his family. God's people seem to stand out through decisions that they make.

Can people around us see a difference between us and the world at large? Do they notice that we're more modest and live simpler lives, that we don't run out and buy something just because we want it? Is it more important to you to be where you can make a lot of money or where you think God wants you to be? Do you spend more time thinking about God or about buying a car, new clothes, or a new stereo system?

Jackson Browne has a song called "The Pretender." It's about a man who began life with great aspirations. He wanted to change things, to do things for people. But his dreams were crushed. All his high ideals plummeted, and he started pursuing material possessions. Listen to what he sings:

> I'm going to be a happy idiot
> And struggle for the legal tender
> Where the ads take aim and lay their claim
> To the heart and soul of the spender,
> And believe in whatever may lie
> In those things that money can buy.
> Thought true love could have been a contender
> Are you there?
> Say a prayer for the pretender
> Who started out so young and strong,
> Only to surrender.

Browne's words show the deceitfulness of money. Many people set out to make money for God's use, but they lose their sense of priorities along the way. We must constantly evaluate our priorities. If you can't sacrifice now with a small bank account, you certainly won't with a big one. You need to start putting some godly principles into your lifestyle now.

Paul gives us four insights about money:

1. *Contentment and simplicity are essential* (1 Timothy 6:6-10). When you start pursuing money outside of godliness, your life will be in trouble. It's godliness with contentment that is great gain. Remember the words of Thoreau: "Simplify, simplify." Or think of Byrd when he was traveling

in the Arctic: "I'm learning that a man can live profoundly without masses of things."

A test you should give yourself before you buy anything is, "Would God want me to use my money for this?" We may have plenty of money, but is that a good reason to buy whatever we desire?

In his book *Celebration of Discipline,* Richard Foster listed ten practical principles for simplifying. These include:

Buy things for their usefulness rather than their status. Apply a bit of healthy skepticism to all "buy now, pay later" schemes. Develop a habit of giving things away. Learn to enjoy things without owning them. Develop a deeper appreciation for things money cannot buy. And shun whatever would distract you from your main goal.

2. Money cannot provide true riches (1 Timothy 6:17 and 18). The rich man thought possessions could provide happiness, so he built larger and larger barns (Luke 12). Jesus said he was a fool, not because he was rich, but because of his view of possessions. They can never make you content.

Philip Yancey described his struggle with money. He said, "I finally got to the point through my writing that I had more money than I really needed." That was one of the worst parts of his life, because money started to occupy him and pull him away from the things he really loved.

Books on investment strategy and tax avoidance tips had supplanted my reading interests in wildlife and classical music. I felt a ceaseless tug to acquire: newer clothes and a bigger house, when those I owned were perfectly adequate; a new car, even though my old one ran fine; a string of investments to accumulate a good nest egg—but for what? Money had become a black hole. The more I had, the more I wanted.

This describes a man with the King Midas phenomenon: if he could just turn things into gold, he thinks, he would be happier. But when he does acquire gold, he loses the best things in life, which the songs say are free. The modern example is Howard Hughes. The classic example from old was Solomon.

If you have ever played a board game called "Life," you will understand the role money plays in our lives. The game is very realistic as you get married, have kids, put them through school, stack up lots of money, and then retire. Each player accumulates money depending on his wise decisions or his luck. Whoever makes the most money wins the game.

The most realistic part, however, comes at the end of the game. Everyone puts his money back in the box when the game of "Life" is over. The board doesn't have a square that symbolizes a funeral, but death is that moment when everyone puts his possessions in the box. It doesn't matter how much or how little we have saved; when our lives are over, someone will take our possessions and put them in a box. It is amazing how much we could learn from this simple game, but most people still don't seem to see why money is not the ultimate priority.

3. *Those with money should use it wisely* (1 Timothy 6:17 and 18). Sometimes we go to the opposite extreme and think it's good to be poor and wrong to be rich. That's not what the text says, however. It doesn't say, "Those of you who are rich, deplete all your resources." It says, "Those of you who are rich, use your money wisely."

Society says the richer you are, the more luxuriously you ought to live. The Bible says the richer you are, the more people you can help. If your gift is contributing to the needs of others, give generously (Romans 12:8).

God blesses some people in his church with the gift of making money so they can bless the world with generosity. Stewardship is the word we usually use. If you have more, you have more to give.

We have members who give 10 percent to the Lord on the average, but is that enough for a rich man to give? One man makes $20,000 a year. Another makes $100,000. The first man lives on $18,000, and the rich man somehow manages to live on $90,000. The question Jesus might ask is, "Which man gave more?" The rich man has the ability to give much more than 10 percent, because he has so much. The temptation he faces is satisfaction with the $10,000 he contributed. The problem is he hasn't sacrificed anything.

He won't miss that money, and he will spend the other $90,000 on himself instead of others.

4. *The kingdom of God, not things, should be central to our lives* (1 Timothy 6:11-16). At the core of our lives should be found, not cars or clothes or stereos, but the kingdom of God. Jesus put it this way: "Seek first the kingdom of God and his righteousness and then all the things you really need will be added to your lives."

Tony Campolo tells of a Mennonite conference debating their historic position that a Christian shouldn't fight in a war. A wealthy old Mennonite gentleman who wanted to be able to protect what he had if anyone invaded his property attacked the position. He was answered by a younger Mennonite. "It's all right for you to talk in this lofty manner," the old gentleman said, "but one of these days they'll come and take everything you have."

The young man responded, "This poses no problem for me. You see, Sir, when I became a Christian, I gave everything I had to Jesus. If they come, they can take from me what belongs to him, and that's his problem."

"All right," the old man responded, "they can't take what you have because you don't have anything, but they can kill you."

The young man answered, "No, they can't. You see, Sir, I'm already dead. When I became a Christian, the life that belongs to this world came to an end, and the new life that I received in Christ can never be snuffed out."

In frustration, the older man said, "They may not be able to take what you have and they may not be able to kill you, but they can make you suffer."

Once again the young man answered, "When that day comes, I hope I will remember the words of Jesus, who said, 'Blessed are those who are persecuted for righteousness' sake, for theirs is the kingdom of heaven.' " There is not much you can do to somebody who doesn't have anything, who's already dead, and who rejoices in persecution!

This young man had it all together! He realized that if the kingdom of God is at the heart of his life, he can use all things to God's glory. We, too, can learn from this example. It's not right or wrong to be rich or poor. But wherever God has placed you in this life, be sure that you possess your things as a steward of God and that they don't possess you. Work to possess the attitude that all things are his, and he allows us to be his custodians.

THOUGHT QUESTIONS FOR CHAPTER 5

1. Do Christians typically live a lifestyle of simplicity and contentment?
2. What can money bring us besides possessions?
3. The writer of Hebrews warned us to remain free from the love of money (Hebrews 13:5 and 6). What does the passage teach us about God that helps produce contentment?
4 Is it possible to be too extravagant in our lifestyle? Would Jesus wear a Rolex watch? Would he drive a Mercedes?
5. Do your teenagers contribute to the church after spending $25.00 on their date Friday night?

ACTIVITY

The leader should have a stack of $1 bills ($50.00 to $100.00).
   a. Pick one teenager to hand the bills to, one at a time.

b. Instruct him to stop you whenever he has enough, but
let him know you will keep going unless he says to stop.

Main point: This will illustrate the hunger we have for
just one more dollar.

CHAPTER 6

Sodom Revisited

Forty years ago in polite circles, you did not talk about homosexuality. Forty years ago the churches did not do much more than consider homosexuals to be sick, perverted criminals. Psychiatrists treated them as any other mental patient, while probably millions of people quietly held questions about their sexual preference.

That started to change in 1948. The Kinsey Report issued that year estimated that 37 per cent of the American males had had at least one homosexual experience. That was probably an inflated figure, but homosexuality was and is a large problem in our country.

In 1955 Sherwin Bailey published a book called *Homosexuality in the Western Tradition* in which he reinterpreted biblical passages to say it's against Western traditions and mores, but not against God's will, to be a homosexual. Bailey's book has become the foundation for homosexual theologians.

In the 1960s the Gay Liberation Movement worked to change attitudes.

In 1968, Troy Perry became the pastor of the first openly homosexual church, the Metropolitan Community Church. In 1972, he wrote the book *The Lord is My Shepherd and He Knows I'm Gay*. Three years later, the Episcopal Church ordained an avowed lesbian to their ministry.

In April of 1985, a homosexual high school opened in New York, paid for largely by local and state dollars.

Today, the problem that is in most of our minds related to homosexuality is AIDS, the mysterious virus that will claim the lives of thousands more because we're incapable of dealing with it at this point. It is rare today to find someone who does not know a gay person. In the next five years it will be unusual not to know someone who has AIDS, which has been so widespread in the homosexual population.

Homosexuality has been defined as a condition in which an individual requires or strongly prefers involvement with members of the same sex. There may be some reading this book who have had a homosexual experience at some point. This experience does not mean you are homosexual, and it does not mean you ever will be. Homosexuality is a part of our culture, and it is a topic that demands sound biblical advice. Let's consider it from the standpoint of four questions.

Question number 1: *What causes someone to become homosexual?* Gary Collins is a psychologist who writes from a Christian perspective. He said,

An increasing body of research would seem to support the idea that homosexuality is not inherited or the result of physiological and biological abnormality. Studies of physical build, chromosomes, neurological or biochemical makeup and even hormones have failed to show differences between homosexuals and heterosexuals. It has been found that while some homosexuals have hormone imbalances, many do not, and a similar hormone imbalance is found in heterosexuals. This has led most researchers to conclude that there is no present evidence to support the idea that homosexuality has a physical or biological cause.

According to Collins, you will usually find certain family

settings in the background of homosexuals. The typical homosexual, he says, might be someone raised in a family with a weak, passive, ineffective father and a domineering mother. In such situations, a son often loses confidence in his masculinity. Or the setting might be one in which mothers distrust or fear other women and teach that distrust to their sons. Another typical background consists of mothers who distrust or fear men and teach their daughters to do the same, or of a son who is surrounded only by females and who consequently learns to think and act like a girl. Still another common setting is one in which parents wanted a daughter but got a son and subtly raised him to think like a girl (or vice versa).

Sometimes a son is rejected by his father and feels inadequate as a male, or a daughter is rejected by her mother and feels inadequate as a female. Often both parents are afraid of sex—and are silent about it in the home except for a strong condemnation of sexual feelings. Children get an imbalanced view of sex when they are raised in any of these situations.

Let's say a child is raised in a family in which stealing is a common event. Both parents steal. His siblings steal. He thinks stealing is a way of life. You cannot say his orientation toward stealing is unusual for that setting. What we can say, however, is that he is still responsible for his own personal behavior. A person who has learned homosexual behavior from his earliest days is not responsible for his orientation any more than a child who is becoming a heterosexual at age ten can be congratulated for those feelings. A child is molded by his environment, which is not in his control. If homosexuality is a learned thing, we cannot blame the twelve-year-old who has grown up in that environment. But we can say that biblically he is responsible for his behavior when he matures, and he can control his environment.

That's where we part company with some behavioral scientists who say you can't go against what you've been taught. Christians believe we can control our behavior! We are enabled by the Holy Spirit to rise above our earthly temptations and live the full life he offers.

The Christian life is best described as a dramatic change in lifestyle. We have moved from darkness into light, and there simply isn't a more stark contrast. Christians believe we can control our behavior, and we believe in a controlled lifestyle. We are all still tempted to sin because we are human, but we choose not to carry out that behavior. Someone may be tempted with homosexual feelings that are just as strong as another's heterosexual feelings. Sin doesn't enter into our lives until we say, "That's just the way I'm made," and give in to the temptation or immorality.

Question number 2: *What does scripture say about homosexuality?* Genesis 1 says nothing about homosexuality, and that's significant. "God created man in his own image. In the image of God he created him. Male and female, he created them" (Genesis 1:27). This is God's intent. He made male and female. He didn't create two males and a female, so Adam could decide which sexual lifestyle he would choose.

In Genesis 2, God gave man a woman. It was Adam and Eve, not Adam and Steve. God's plan for sexual fulfillment was a marriage between a husband and wife that was to last forever.

Genesis 19 tells of the sin of Sodom. We are told earlier in Genesis that Sodom's wickedness is serious. "Now the men of Sodom were wicked and were sinning greatly against the Lord" (Genesis 13:13). "Then the Lord said, 'The outcry against Sodom and Gomorrah is so great and their sins so grievous that I will go down and see if what they have done is as bad as the outcry that has reached me. If not, I will know' " (Genesis 18:20 and 21).

He sent his messengers to the city, and when they had eaten and were about to retire, all the men of the city gathered around Lot's house and started screaming, "Bring out the men that we may know them."

Bailey claimed this means only that the men of the city wanted to become acquainted with the messengers. They were a sort of local Welcome Wagon. His evidence for that interpretation was that of the 943 occurrences of *yadhah* ("know") in the Old Testament, only fourteen are clearly sexual.

The determination of a word's meaning, however, comes from its context and not from stacking up numbers of occurrences. "Know" in verse 8 clearly is sexual. It is in verse 5 as well: "We want to have sexual intercourse with the men in your house." The passage stands as a clear condemnation of homosexual activity (cf. Jude 7).

In the New Testament, Paul wrote:

Do you not know that the wicked will not inherit the kingdom of God? Do not be deceived: Neither the sexually immoral nor idolaters nor adulterers nor male prostitutes nor homosexual offenders nor thieves nor the greedy nor drunkards nor slanderers nor swindlers will inherit the kingdom of God (1 Corinthians 6:9 and 10).

Finally, the book of Romans tells us that the wrath of God was poured out on mankind because of its wickedness:

Because of this, God gave them over to the shameful lusts. Even their women exchanged natural relations for unnatural ones. In the same way the men also abandoned natural relations with women and were inflamed with lust for one another. Men committed indecent acts with other men, and received in themselves the due penalty for their perversion (Romans 1:26).

Those who are practicing acts of homosexuality are condemned by God. It is a sin that can cause you to lose your soul if you do not correct it. God is blunt without being crude, but it would be hard to misunderstand these verses.

Question number 3: *What should the church's response be to homosexuality?* Two words come to mind, confrontation and compassion. The spirit of the age today says, "I don't have any right to be involved in your life whether you're a Christian or not. You have the right to choose your lifestyle." As one woman's lawyer said in Oklahoma, "I don't care if she fornicates up one side of the street and down the other; it's none of the church's business."

That's the spirit of the age and of the "Phil Donahue Show," but it is NOT the spirit of New Testament Christianity. Loving is vital to the New Testament, but not a weak, mushy love. It's a tough love that at times must confront. If I love you and believe what Paul said about homosexuality costing your soul, love will *lead* me to confrontation. If someone's child were about to walk into danger, I wouldn't think it was none of my business. I would prevent him from hurting himself, and I think you would do the same. We *must* show even more concern for our friends' spiritual welfare. If we see them living a destructive lifestyle, we are called to confront them.

One way to confront homosexuality is to call it by its real name. The homosexual population likes to use terms like "alternate lifestyle" or "different sexual orientation." Those sound very fashionable, but God calls it "sin."

Another way to confront this practice is to teach God's plan for our sexuality. Parents should model this lifestyle for their children. Even single parents can share a positive sexual approach to their children.

The second word is compassion. Some Christians need to repent because they have stereotyped people. They have felt that anyone with an effeminate voice is homosexual or that all homosexuals walk the streets looking for little boys to seduce.

Homosexuals need compassion, understanding, and help rather than condemnation and rejection. The main reason we don't have compassion is that we don't understand. We find the idea repulsive, which lowers our compassion level. The church is commanded to love people who have been trapped by sin. God's love is the quality that should attract a lost world into our buildings. We must not treat homosexuals like modern-day lepers. We need to repent of our attitudes toward those who struggle with homosexuality.

It is interesting the sins God puts with the sin of homosexuality. In Romans 1:29-32 Paul says:

They have become filled with every kind of wickedness, evil, greed and depravity. They are full of envy, murder, strife, deceit and malice. They are gossips, slanderers, God-haters, insolent, arrogant and boastful; they invent ways of doing evil; they disobey their parents; they are senseless, faithless, heartless, ruthless. Although they know God's righteous decree that those who do such things deserve death, they not only continue to do these very things but also approve of those who practice them.

I wonder how many of these sins have touched your life? I'm sure everyone is obeying their parents at all times! We need to be careful in making homosexuality a major sin, and then considering our many sins as just minor misdemeanors. The end result of envy, sexual immorality, hatred, and gossip is the same—those who live like this will *not* inherit the kingdom of God (Galatians 5:21).

When Jesus met a sinful woman, he didn't condone her actions, but was understanding. He tried to minister to her (Luke 7:36-50). Some saw her as a social leper. They saw what she had been, but Jesus saw what she could be. She knew the one man in that room who would love her, and his compassion drew her to him.

God calls the church to the same ministry. We can't minister to people we stereotype and write off. Homosexuals need love. The old saying is still valid: "Hate the sin, but love the sinner." Loving confrontation mingled with compassion should characterize the church.

In 1988 I asked Lynn Anderson to write an article for *20th Century Christian* magazine based on his congregation's compassionate response to a man dying of AIDS. Following is that penetrating story, used by permission:

When I saw Don moving tentatively down the aisle toward me I felt a knot of anxiety gathering in my stomach. He had told me he would be coming—but why did he have to choose this particular day?

Don handed me his card. The invitation song ended, and the crowd sat down—except for Don, who stood beside me, turning to face the audience. I cleared my throat and glanced at the card: "My name is Don Peables. I am a Christian—baptized in Odessa, Texas in 1969 at the 5th and Jackson Church of Christ. *I am an AIDS victim!* I would like to confess my sins publicly and rededicate my life to the Lord. I would like to place my membership here."

The knot in my stomach drew tighter. No, it wasn't the AIDS I was afraid of. This was homecoming Sunday at A.C.U. Our Sunday morning assembly was packed with guests from all over the nation. How would they handle Don? As they returned to dozens of cities, what would they say about us—the Highland church?

Don was no stranger. We knew he had AIDS. Also, some from our church had already confronted AIDS in their own families. The Highland church had published a tabloid on AIDS—circulating it not only in the church family, but in the city of Abilene as well. The tabloid contained articles written by psychologists, medical doctors, sex therapists and ministers, calling for a compassionate and redemptive response to persons with AIDS—attempting to dispel the hysteria and fear triggered by misinformation.

Don had read this piece and had visited our church to hear a sermon on "AIDS—A Christian Response." I had then visited in Don's home, heard him confess and weep, prayed with him and offered him help. One of our deacons, Dr. Gordon Golden, a physician, had already ministered to Don, helping him obtain the AZT medication he needed. Church funds had covered some of the costs.

But now—on this homecoming Sunday morning, with all those visitors present, Don stood conspicuously in the center of our worship assembly, asking to be part of us—to belong!

I was not completely sure how our own Highland people would respond to him—even after the orientation they had been through. And all those visitors! What *was* I to except from strangers—especially in the volatile climate which had, a few weeks earlier, burned down the home of a Florida family whose clear-eyed young sons—hemophiliacs—had contracted AIDS?

However, we had opened the door and had prepared our people and our community the best we could.

So I slid my arm around Don's shoulders and read the card aloud to the whole mixed bag of people. Then I put both arms around Don, embraced him—hard—and welcomed him into the Highland fellowship. I assured Don that we were his family and would never leave him—but would be with him until he died.

Just before we spoke a benediction, our elders invited the crowd to come down front and meet Don and assure him our words were genuine.

What a morning! After the dismissal prayer, people flowed up the aisles—waiting in line to join those who embraced Don and spoke words of love and promise to him. Don was captive to the crowd for more than thirty minutes after the service. What a Sunday! It was a day, fashioned by the love of God, in which to rejoice and be glad.

But that Sunday morning was not the end of the story. In fact, homecoming Sunday merely marked the beginning of the church family's response to Don.

Christian doctors and nurses gave Don medical care. Christians representing all age groups continued visiting him, driving him to doctors' offices, running errands for him and nurturing his self-esteem. Two graduate students led Bible studies with Don and his roommate.

As the illness progressed, food brigades brought home-cooked meals, hand delivered daily to Don's door. A number of families prayed with Don regularly in his sick-room. Some took their children to meet Don, and the children sang around his bed.

Oh, blessed and redemptive community of faith! Oh, wise plan of Adonai!

Don is gone now. His death came slow and hard. He lived nearly three years after diagnosis—longer than most AIDS patients. But Don often said that he thanked God for AIDS, because it gave him time to "get his life in order" before he died.

Don's funeral was attended by three groups of people: a number of friends from the gay community, a strong delegation of brothers and sisters in Christ, and a cadre of reporters from the news media.

As I spoke frail words to the family, looking into their pained faces, I could see comfort rising in their eyes. I also saw a look of gratitude growing toward the family of God—I think toward God himself. In the eyes of others who came to mourn, I think I saw hysteria melt away and hope spring to life.

We reflected that day, with that strange gathering, on lepers, ancient and modern—and on how Jesus stretched out his hand

and touched the lepers, not only risking social rejection but laying his life on the line. In so doing, he cast his lot with those poor disenfranchised waifs, giving personhood and healing to those who had been regarded as accursed.

In Christ we "no longer view people from a wordly point of view" (2 Corinthians 5:8).

News media covered Don's funeral procession. In the *Abilene Reporter News,* among the other kind columns, the following letter appeared:

> I wish to commend . . . Highland Church of Christ for their assistance to the late Don Peables, an Abilenian who had the courage to publicly admit that he had AIDS.
>
> In attending Don, the members of Highland were actually living out their Christianity. They provided food on a regular basis, secured him needed equipment, and most important, gave him warm, personal concern. This is precisely the kind of response demanded of churches of all denominations to the families stricken by AIDS.

"By this shall all men know that you are my disciples, because you have love for one another."

Question number 4: *How can the homosexual bring his life under control?* If you're struggling with homosexuality, you *can* control your behavior. It's hard, but it can be done. It's hard for alcoholics to quit drinking—painfully hard. Sometimes they want to be tied down on a bed to keep them from getting another drink. It's hard for someone who's been promiscuous heterosexually for years to stop. What about people who've been stealing all their lives? Do you know how hard it is for them to quit?

It's difficult to change, but I refuse to buy into the teaching of those who say you can't change. The Bible tells us that God has all power; he can help us develop self-control.

Let me suggest five steps toward recovery. They are painful, difficult, long-term steps, but people have given testimony that with God's help they have become nonpracticing homosexuals.

1. *Admit That It's A Sin*

As long as you keep fooling yourself, you have no way to overcome any sin. People who struggle with homosexuality know the guilt involved with it. Guilt causes us to hide our sins in darkness, yet Jesus asks us to confess our sins to break the bond of guilt (James 5:16). As Paul said, "No temptation has seized you except what is common to man. And God is faithful; he will not let you be tempted beyond what you can bear" (1 Corinthians 10:13). It isn't that there's no temptation. If you've grown up with that learned behavior, you'll probably be tempted to the day you die, but there will never come a temptation that you cannot choose to combat and overcome by the power of God. Jesus doesn't bring guilt. He brings hope!

2. *Trust In The Lord*

I'm not talking about singing or proclaiming that we ought to trust him. We all know that. I mean really turning your life over to him in submission.

There's a being more powerful than we are, and we *must* rely on him. Homosexuality is a spiritual battle, and we fight it with spiritual weapons (Ephesians 6).

God has a great record. He could take a little boy named David and go up against Goliath. He could take Gideon with 300 men and go up against the myriads of Midianite soldiers. He could take a man with demons and send him to a new life. Homosexuality, like demon-possession, is an overwhelming experience calling for outside help. That help is from God Almighty!

3. *Break Away From the Homosexual Environment*

You must break all connections with things that encourage a homosexual orientation. The use of pornography must be stopped, and all homosexual friendships must end. This is a radical change, but it will be crucial to your deliverance from this problem. There will be a need to find new friends and new activities to fill your time. This is where the church can be very vital in filling a need for support.

If you're young, don't experiment. Don't play with fire. If you've grown up in environments where you have questions about your orientation, be assured that what God said is true. He made us male and female. Don't change his plan. If you have already had homosexual experiences, don't do it again.

The mind is not a vacuum. You can't remove all those things and leave it empty. You've got to put new things in. If you don't, you'll go back to your old ways of thinking and acting. Read new material. Find new friends. Associate as much as you can with God's church.

4. *Be Accountable to a Trusted Christian*

That doesn't mean you have to walk down the aisle, fill out a card, and tell the whole community, but share it with somebody whom you deeply trust, like your minister or a Christian counselor. Then listen to his advice.

5. *Believe There is Hope*

If you don't believe there's hope, there won't be for you. If you believe you're trapped and there's no way out, you're fighting a losing battle. Jesus can deliver you from any sin, and he will give you the strength to break Satan's control.

THOUGHT QUESTIONS FOR CHAPTER 6

1. What barriers make it difficult for a youth group to confront and be compassionate to homosexuals?

2. Why is homosexual sin considered worse than greed or drunkenness? (1 Corinthians 6:9 and 10).

3. Do you believe AIDS is the penalty sent by God in Romans 1:26?

4. Do you think society has accepted homosexuality as an alternate lifestyle? Why?

5. If a homosexual man confessed his sin before the church, how would your church respond? If he had AIDS, how would they respond?

CHAPTER 7

The Dating Game

This is an odd way to begin a chapter on dating, but I have to say it: dating is overrated!

Oh, I know dating is wonderful. That male/female attraction goes back at least to third grade when you sent that letter: "I love you. Do you love me? Check one: _____ yes _____ no." When your dating life is great you feel great all over.

But, when you get dropped or when you aren't asked out or when you're turned down, you feel awful. So many teenagers stay depressed and lonely because of an unpleasant— or fossilized—dating life.

Our first and ultimate commitment isn't to dating but to Jesus. You are valuable because he thinks you are valuable. Even if you never date (and many teens never do), even if you remain single all your life, you can be "whole." Our new sense of worth comes from following Jesus and not from being asked out.

When we do date, though, we must maintain a Christian perspective, not conforming to all the world's games (Romans 12:1 and 2). While this chapter is about dating and not marriage, the two topics overlap. The tragedy of broken homes forces us to think seriously about how we date.

The *Miami Herald* might have lost an incredible wedding

story, if the couple whose wedding they covered had not made dating just a game. The reporter tells about this event.

A young British couple decided to get a divorce while their wedding reception was still in progress. Daniel and Susan Stockwell had barely started the reception before they had a furious argument that was apparently spurred when the bride saw the groom talking to an ex-girlfriend. "I must have been mad to go through with it!" London's *Daily Merit* newspaper quoted the groom as saying. "I'm better off without her."

Wow! Isn't it incredible that some people treat marriage like a game! Many teens treat dating like a game. The rules in the game are: don't let anyone hurt you, always break up with him/her first, and hang on to your guy or girl only until someone better comes along. Basically, this attitude promotes the idea of "everyone for himself," which is an attitude totally contrary to God's plan. We must not overlook this important stage of your life. The biggest reason is that your marriage partner will be found in this process. I want to look at God's plan for marriage and hope to give you some hints on how to choose a Christian husband or wife.

Disposable Marriages

Chuck Swindoll mentioned a sign at a Hollywood pawn shop that said, "We rent wedding rings." Why not? If you aren't going to use it more than a year or two, it would be foolish to pay hundreds or thousands of dollars for a wedding ring. Maybe you could rent with an option to buy later!

At some wedding ceremonies, the words "as long as we both shall live" have been replaced with "as long as we both shall love." Many don't want to enter into contracts for life. Maybe for love, but not for life. For all practical purposes, "until death do we part" has been replaced with "for three years, at which time we'll renegotiate." These couples don't want a life-long commitment.

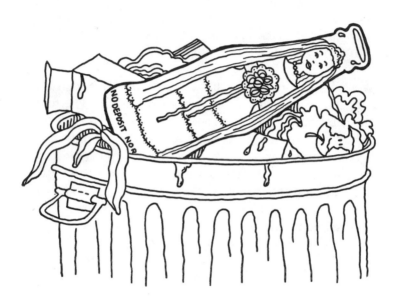

The devastation of divorce has even infiltrated into the ranks of Christians. We used to say that ninety-nine per cent of the marriages contracted at Christian colleges lasted. We can't say that anymore.

Some who are single may think of marriage as a good thing to try. Notice: *something to try.* If it doesn't work out, just discard it and try again. It's like disposable diapers. Use them, dispose of them, and buy more. There just aren't many things that our society expects to last a lifetime, especially a marriage.

God demands that we stand against the cultural tide. We must try to transform culture rather than just ride along with it. Our views of marriage need to be carved out of Scripture and out of Jesus' view of marriage regardless of what they're doing on "L.A. Law," what a Gallup Poll says, or what *People* magazine advocates. As Paul states in Romans 12:1 and 2, we must be "transformed" (different) from the world and its views.

Of course, you can be divorced and still be a faithful Christian. You don't have to be a second-class citizen in God's kingdom just because you're divorced. God loves all his children, and he heals all wounds. Some of the most sensitive, compassionate people in the world are people who have been divorced. They, too, would probably be the first to say that divorce isn't God's plan for marriage. The trials and upheavals they experienced cannot be God's plan. If you watched the movie "Kramer vs. Kramer," you felt the pain of divorce. The hearts of America broke as they saw the dark side of this situation. The actors and actresses did a great job in the movie, but this is real life for families that you know. God never wants you to experience the agony of a divorce, so we *must* listen to his words concerning marriage and dating in order to avoid this tragedy

God's Design for Marriage

God brought Adam and Eve together and said to Adam, "Cleave to your wife. Be united with her." There's something permanent about that. God wasn't saying, "Adam, try Eve for a while and then start looking around." For one thing, the pickin's were pretty slim at that time! Rather, God said, "Cleave to her. Stay with her." God wants one man and one woman united for life. God's design for marriage is a permanent bond.

Let me try to illustrate this with two separate sheets of paper. One sheet represents man and the other sheet represents woman. God commands them to cleave or bond only to each other. We put glue on the sheets and press them together. The glue dries, and the bond becomes stronger as time passes. This is symbolic of the time a couple spends together in a marriage. Each day makes that bond stronger. Now, what would happen if I asked you to pull the sheets apart? You would tear each sheet of paper in several places. God knows how destructive that is to both people in a marriage. Imagine repeating this illustration several times, like so many people do with their marriages. What is left of the piece of paper that was man? Woman? It is literally torn to shreds.

God's design for marriage was simple. Cleave to each other even during the hard times. The life of Hosea illustrates this point well. Hosea had what we call a scriptural reason for divorce. His wife had left him. She was an adulteress. She was unfaithful, but Hosea still wanted her back. Just because adultery is involved doesn't mean you *have to divorce*. That's how sacred marriage was to God and to Hosea. God was saying to Hosea, "Go out and find your wife again and bring her back" (Hosea 3:1). And Hosea did! He loved her in spite of the hurt that she had caused, and he obeyed God's will for his marriage.

There was a generation during the days of Malachi that became very corrupt. Divorce was commonplace. The poor were oppressed, so Malachi let them know how God feels about broken marriages.

Another thing you do: You flood the Lord's altar with tears. You weep and wail because he no longer pays attention to your offerings or accepts them with pleasure from your hands. You ask, "Why?" It is because the Lord is acting as the witness between you and the wife of your youth, because you have broken faith with her, though she is your partner, the wife of your marriage covenant. Has not the Lord made them one? In flesh and spirit they are his. And why one? Because he was seeking godly offspring. So guard yourself in your spirit, and do not break faith with the wife of your youth. "I hate divorce," says the Lord God of Israel . . . (Malachi 2:13-16).

There aren't a lot of ways to interpret that. God hates divorce. Despite all the exceptions we might talk about and the special cases we might come up with, the bottom line is God's design, beginning in Genesis and continuing through Malachi: God wants marriage to be permanent.

Jesus reiterated the emphasis on permanence. Loophole lawyers are always looking for an "out," an excuse why this doesn't apply. But Jesus didn't negotiate with loophole lawyers. He said, "Yes, fornication is a way of breaking the bond." But he returned to the heart of long-term commitment:

"Haven't you read," he replied, "that at the beginning the Creator 'made them male and female,' and said, 'For this reason a man will leave his father and mother and be united to his wife, and the two will become one flesh'? So they are no longer two, but one. Therefore what God has joined together, let man not separate" (Matthew 19:4-6).

Finally, Paul used marriage as an illustration when he said:

For example, by law a married woman is bound to her husband as long as he is alive, but if her husband dies, she is released from the

77

law of marriage. So then, if she marries another man while her husband is still alive, she is called an adulteress. But if her husband dies, she is released from that law and is not an adulteress, even though she marries another man (Romans 7:2 and 3).

God wants marriage to last for life. There will be ups and downs, but he wants us to stay in there with stubborn love. Look at God's design for marriage. God has always said, "I want people to stay married for life."

If we're going to be God's people, we have to find a way for our marriages to last and be a light to the world. A major reason marriages don't last is that partners chose the wrong person to marry. I know too many girls who aren't looking for Mr. Right. They will settle for Mr. Right Now. I would propose that you set some standards for the people you will date. Qualifications should be set before you even begin to date. It is so easy to fall in love and realize later that love blinded you to some major flaws. Most marriage counselors know that when a couple decides to get married, they can't hear anything except wedding bells.

Dating is an exciting phase of life, but it also can cause lots of worries. Do you remember your first date? Remember the stomach full of butterflies? Deborah Retzky captures those feelings in this short story called "First Date."

I wipe my hands on my new corduroys and straighten my collar. Okay. Now all I have to do is walk up to the door, and we'll be on our way. I pick up the newspaper and ring the doorbell. Did I ring it hard enough? Should I press it again? No. Someone is running to the door. I hear sneakers squeaking on the linoleum.

"Who is it?" pipes a little voice from within.

"It's Eric," I answer, my voice croaking as usual. I wipe my hands on my pants.

"Who?" the voice asks again.

I wonder if I should flee from the scene, but I answer, "Eric." The door is opened by a woman I assume is my date's mother. Lauren's little sister is hiding behind her mother's legs, looking at me closely. The woman smiles and holds out her hand.

"I'm Lauren's mother," she says.

I take her hand and say, "Pleased to meet you, Mrs. Halverson."

I hand her the newspaper I picked up. She has cool palms, and I become aware that my own hand is sticky.

I am relieved to see Lauren appear. She orders her little sister to leave the room.

"Shall we go?" Lauren asks me.

The movie theater is not far. We have time before the first show, so we walk slowly. On the way I invent a way to wipe my palms on my pants without being obvious.

I watch Lauren out of the corner of my eye. She is very calm and is dressed nicely. I hope I won't spill buttered popcorn on her lap. That is sure to happen, though. I don't think it's fair that she's so calm. Why should guys be the only ones to worry over a date?

Soon we are settled in our seats with a large carton of popcorn between us. I begin to relax—until I remember that she probably expects me to hold her hand.

Okay. Count to ten. One, two, three. . . .

"Would you like some more popcorn?" I chicken out.

"No, thanks."

So much for conversation. But we are at a movie, after all, and I feel I have to do something. I stretch my legs and arms. I eat more popcorn. When it is gone, I put the carton on the floor.

Then I take a deep breath. One, two, three, four, five, six, seven, eight, nine, nine and a half, nine and three quarters, . . . ten. I lean over to take her hand, and she lets me. Miracle of miracles, her hand is sweaty, too!

Dating is such an exciting time in life, but I would encourage you to set some standards for your dates. Don't settle for second best. Listed below are a few suggestions for you to keep in mind in your dating relationships.

1. *Keep Your Relationship Centered on God.* I listed this one first for a reason. The person you date seriously or plan to marry should bring you closer to God. There are two basic groups you can date—Christians and non-Christians. I think you will find it hard to keep your relationship God-centered with a non-Christian.

I know several girls who made dating their ministry. They found the worst guys in school and began "mission-trip" dating. They felt with a little love even the worst guys could change. One of these girls would start dating a guy, then she would drag this young man to church for several weeks against his will. He wasn't into this religious stuff. Then the relationship would slowly begin to pull her away from God. Quite honestly, I have seen ten times more girls lost than guys led to the Lord through "mission-trip" dating. I encourage you to find a person who is committed to the Lord. Look for someone who can pray with you during your dates. Don't look for a guy who prays that you're not pregnant after your date.

Don't be fooled by the qualities the world holds up as important. Don't fall in love with beauty, athletic ability or money. Those are things that can be lost in an instant. One car wreck or one disease can take these things away. Besides, time usually causes beauty and athletic ability to fade. When a person is growing in the Lord, time doesn't weaken this spirituality; it strengthens it. The car accident doesn't eliminate the commitment, rather it stimulates their faith.

Ask yourself these three questions: Do I see Jesus in this person? Does this person have a deep prayer life? Does this person bring me closer or pull me farther away from God?

Another question you must ask yourself is: Can people see

my commitment to Jesus through my life? This will determine what type of people will be attracted to you.

2. *Find Someone Who Loves in Spite of How They Feel.* We're in trouble if we date with love as a feeling because feelings are fickle. Most of the time they're good and warm, but other times they aren't. You can't rely on them. I think Jim Long described this situation well in this poem.

IF LOVE WERE JUST A FEELING

Like a hot shot
on a new-car shopping spree,
I'd check out your equipment,
If love were just a feeling.
I'd fixate on all the externals:
the shape of your body,
the style of your talk,
perhaps your humor and your poise.
I'd judge by what I see, hear, touch,
touch,
if love were just a feeling.

Like two mannequins
sharing a display case in silence.
I'd never really know you.
I'd ignore your humanness,
deny your faults, too, perhaps.
But I'd also exploit you,
taking what you have,
what I want,
if love were just a feeling.

Like Swedish ivy intertwined,
I'd cling to you possessively.
And smothering you,
I'd make our already superficial relationship
more shallow still,
if love were just a feeling.

Like a sportsman
shooting white-water rapids,
I'd conquer you and move on.
Our relationship would surge,
invigorating but temporary.
There would be nothing to hold me
when the exhilarating gave way
to the commonplace,
or the inevitable conflicts came
if, for me, love were just a feeling.
—by Jim Long

When you get married, you won't always have a mushy feeling in your stomach. When Paul said, "Husbands, love your wives," he wasn't saying have a romantic feeling 365 days a year. He was telling us to make a decision that we're going to love.

Jesus said for us to love our enemies (Matthew 5). He wasn't saying to have tickly feelings on the inside about them. He was calling for a basic commitment of good will toward them.

We need the kind of committed love expressed in a note Charlie Shedd's wife left him after an argument: "Dear Charlie, I hate you. Love, Martha." We who are married can identify!

You can't always deal with the emotions, but you can deal with decisions. "I've decided I'm going to love you. Even on days we don't feel particularly close, I'm going to act lovingly toward you." And as you act that way, the feelings will eventually follow. You're not trying to do something against your will. You want to love. You want to make that commitment for life. That's a healthy view of love.

When you decide to really love someone, it takes your

relationship off the rollercoaster. Don't you hate riding the ups and downs of someone else's emotions? One minute he worships the ground you walk on, and the next day you are the lowest form of life. One day you spend four hours on the phone, and the next day you get the silent treatment. If you really want a tough test, read 1 Corinthians 13:4-8. Look at the qualities in that list. Place your boyfriend or girlfriend's name where love is written in the passage. If it doesn't sound correct, you aren't dating the right one.

3. *Find Someone Who Zeroes in on Your Positive Qualities.* Paul in his epistles always began by talking about things for which he was thankful. He was almost always writing to correct something, but he began with something positive. Even in his first epistle to the Corinthians, when he could hardly think of anything good to say, he thanked God for "the grace that is evident among you." God was working among them whether they knew it or not.

We, too, should focus on the positive qualities. Look for the good things in your boyfriend or girlfriend. What drew you together in the first place? Before you dated he seemed so decisive, and you liked that. Now he seems pigheaded. It's the same quality from a different perspective!

How much do you like being around a negative thinker? How many of you like to hear your faults announced to the general public? Now, how would you like being married to a negative spouse who knows all your faults? Your boyfriend should compliment you in front of others rather than cut you down. Your girlfriend should praise your good qualities rather than make fun of your bad ones.

4. *Avoid Situations that Hinder the Relationship.* The greatest hindrance to many Christian young couples is sexual activity. I see many active Christian teenagers go steady, and I enjoy watching them grow closer together. After several months, though, sometimes I begin to see danger signs. They begin to fight more with each other, and their attendance at church falls dramatically.

I have found that most couples who show these signs are involved in sexual activity or are very close to it. The fights are caused by differences in sexual standards, and the drop in church attendance is caused by guilt. They feel very uncomfortable at church, especially when the subject is sexual purity.

There is a book called *Too Close Too Soon* written by Jim Talley and Bobbie Reed. It was written with single adults in mind, but I think there is a solid point for teenagers. Their research indicates that a dating couple that spends 300 hours of intimate time together will be sexually active. They are not talking about total time spent together within a group situation. They are talking about one on one intimate unchaperoned time.

I see many teen couples who spend so much time together they could hit 300 hours within three months. They seem to also have the most trouble remaining faithful to God's sexual standards. A relationship should be a gradual process. The slower pace will keep the friendship growing and will also help fight against sexual temptation.

If you are currently involved in sexual activity, it isn't too late to stop. The first step is to be accountable to a trusted adult. The couple needs to find some adult who can offer good advice and check on their progress. Accountability is good for every Christian no matter what his or her age.

The next step is to avoid the empty houses and dark secluded roads. Spend more time with groups of your peers. If you struggle with temptation, I promise you won't have a sexual thought with fifteen people in your Toyota. You need to carefully decide what situations will not invite sexual temptation.

Your dating life will determine your mate for a lifetime. It isn't something you want to take lightly. Hopefully, you will set some guidelines for your dates, and you will find a beautiful Christian wife or husband to marry. I pray your mate will be dedicated to the Lord first and foremost, and I pray you will be a generation that honors the words "until death do you part."

THOUGHT QUESTIONS FOR CHAPTER 7

1. Should a Christian date a non-Christian? Why?
2. What are the bad effects of divorce on the kids?
3. Why did God want us to stay with the same person all of our lives?
4. Ask the guys to list qualities they will look for in a wife. (Prioritize them.)
5. Ask the girls to list qualities they will look for in a husband. (Prioritize them.)
6. List some sexually tempting situations for couples.
7. List some healthy situations that keep the couple accountable.

ACTIVITY

1. Glue two plain white sheets of paper together. Wait about 5 minutes. Instruct a student to carefully separate the two sheets.
   Discuss how this is symbolic of divorce.
2. Involve students in a roleplay of a dating situation. The boyfriend should ask the girl to go parking on a desolate road. Let the girl show how she would flee from this situation.

CHAPTER 8

Chumming the Waters

My first experience trolling for king mackerel off the East Coast was like a chapter out of some exotic fairytale. My wife, Diane, and I were with our good friends, Joe and Kathy Mattox, in their comfortable boat. The weather was gorgeous: bright sun, soft breeze, gentle waves. It was the kind of day where you almost hope the fish will leave you alone.

When Joe invited me to go tournament fishing with him, I thought that since it was so much fun on just a regular day, there was no telling how much fun a tournament would be. But an amazing transformation can come over a man when you pass from a regular, mess-around day to a bona fide tournament day. Laid Back, Who-Cares-If-You-Miss-One Joe turns into Joe the Fishing Fanatic.

We got up before intelligent people normally do and went up and down the Intracoastal Waterway looking for baitfish. On a nontournament day any baitfish will do, but on a tournament day it has to be menhaden, about six inches long—just what a mackerel is looking for when it's hungry. When we found them flipping in the water, Joe threw the net and hauled in three or four hundred fish, enough for the day.

On the previous day, we'd gotten about the same number of menhaden and had fed them into a meat grinder. You can imagine how much fun that was—for me and the menhaden! You can also imagine the smell the next morning after it sat out half-frozen the previous night. This manhaden mush was put in a sack and became our chum bag. Now with the chum bag plus the live menhaden, out we went to the ocean. This time there was no sun shining and the waves were nasty as we headed seaward forty or fifty miles.

When we finally reached *the* spot, we tossed the chum bag out. Then we began trolling around it in circles. But to make the area even more enticing to a king mackerel, we (actually—I) continued dicing the live menhaden into thirds and tossing the pieces behind the boat as fresh chum. That ranks on the excitement scale right up there with changing a baby's diapers and having a cavity filled.

With the chum bag out and fresh chunks of menhaden in the water, there is often a feeding frenzy. Word gets out that there are freebies floating on the water's surface, and every mackerel and shark within a wide radius show up for a meal. (The similarities to a high school student taking a pizza into the school cafeteria are striking.) Up come the mackerel, and if you're lucky, they start hitting the bait on your line.

This method of fishing is similar to a style of evangelism Paul described:

But thanks be to God, who always leads us in triumphal procession in Christ and through us spreads everywhere the fragrance of the knowledge of him. For we are to God the aroma of Christ among those who are being saved and those who are perishing. To the one we are the smell of death; to the other, the fragrance of life. And who is equal to such a task? Unlike so many, we don't peddle the word of God for profit. On the contrary, in Christ we speak before God with sincerity, like men sent from God (2 Corinthians 2:14-17).

The two concepts we're considering in this study of Christ and culture are holiness and ministry. The first seven chapters centered on holiness—how we can be distinct in our values from the world. The remaining chapters concern our ministry—how we change a world in darkness with the light of the Gospel, how we identify without becoming identical, and how we function as fishers of men.

A Chum Bag for the World

We serve as chum—a chum bag that's set out for the world. Not a very glamorous position, is it? Thomas Kempis said, "God has lots of people who are yearning for the kingdom, but not nearly so many who are willing to bear the cross."

One of my favorite religious novels was written by Sheldon VanAuken. He and his wife, Davie, considered themselves "high pagans." They were not believers, but they lived fairly moral lives. After they moved to England and began rubbing elbows with C. S. Lewis, they came to believe that Jesus was who he claimed to be. In his book *A Severe Mercy*, VanAuken reflected on the conversion process:

The best argument for Christianity is Christians: their joy, their certainty, their completeness. But the strongest argument against Christianity is also Christians—when they are somber and joyless, when they are self-righteous and smug in complacent consecration, when they are narrow and repressive, then Christianity dies a thousand deaths.

We must be the best bait in order to attract the most fish. If you have claimed Christ, you're part of the bait. The question is, "What kind of bait are you?" God isn't looking for stale, lifeless chum that will be ignored. He is looking for people who are full of life and full of Christ.

The reason fish like chum is that it fills a need they have. They have a need for food to fill empty stomachs, so they search for sources that fill that particular need.

Jesus fills man's ultimate need. Man was separated from God by sin (Romans 3:23). Man couldn't cross the void that sin caused, so Jesus had to be the perfect sacrifice. Jesus became our best example of chum. He sacrificed his very life in order to bring mankind back to God.

When Jesus came to this earth, the world was in a state of religious confusion. Hypocrisy was rampant. When Jesus stepped into the religious scene, he didn't just bring teaching about grace and truth—he was grace and truth in action. When you touched him, you were touching mercy; you were touching love; love like you had never felt before. He was a breath of fresh air in a smug and stale religious community. Jesus filled the people's needs through his teaching, his healing, and his compassion. He gave their lives purpose and meaning. Jesus saw them wandering in darkness, and the people saw Jesus as their light.

He does that same thing today. He is the same today as he was yesterday, and he still offers light to the world. We *must* share this light with the dark world around us.

Paul discussed how to minister to a culture that is different from yours in his first letter to the church at Thessalonica:

Make it your ambition to lead a quiet life, to mind your own business and to work with your hands, just as we told you, so that your daily life may win the respect of outsiders and so that you will not be dependent on anybody (1 Thessalonians 4:11 and 12).

Some Christians don't worry what the world thinks about them, but Paul makes it crystal clear that we have a responsibility to earn respect. We won't attract anyone if they don't have respect for us. How do we win this respect? Live like Christ, and you will find people attracted to your unconditional love. They will be drawn to your compassion.

But how do you react when people persecute you? Do you fight back? Give up on your faith? Peter wrote to encourage Christians who are being slandered:

Dear friends, I urge you, as aliens and strangers in the world, to abstain from sinful desires, which war against your soul. Live such good lives among the pagans that, though they accuse you of doing wrong, they may see your good deeds and glorify God on the day he visits us (1 Peter 2:11 and 12).

Peter continued by encouraging Christians to obey the law, to put in a good day's work, to accept any persecution that comes. He told wives of non-Christians to demonstrate the beauty of knowing Christ, to be submissive, to keep serving and loving. He told husbands not to treat their wives as second-class citizens, but to be considerate of them and fill them with self-esteem. And he told everyone not to bicker, but to live in harmony and repay evil with good.

When your life reflects Jesus, someone will ask you about the hope you have. At that point, very gently, you tell him about Jesus.

The Universal Attraction

What one quality will attract the world to Jesus? What quality shows that we are following Christ? "By this all men will know that you are my disciples, if you love one another" (John 13:35). I know teenagers who decided to give church a try, but they never experienced the love that Christ wanted them to feel. They may have been rejected because they didn't fit the mold of the youth group. They may not have fit because they didn't go to the right school. These kids simply were not shown love as Christ commanded it. They felt they didn't need Christians because Christians were no different from the world. We need to take advantage of each opportunity we get to help people who are searching for love.

Truman Dollar and Grace Ketterman in their book

Teenage Rebellion, included this article from a recent periodical.

The phone rang in a fashionable suburban home. "Hi, Mom, I'm coming home."

A serviceman in San Diego had just returned from active duty. His mother was wild with joy. Her boy was alive.

"I'm bringing a buddy with me," he said. "He got hurt pretty bad. Only has one eye, one arm, and one leg. He has no home, and I'd like him to live with us."

"Sure, Son," the mother said. "He can stay with us for a while."

"Mom, you don't understand. I want him to live with us always."

"Well, okay," the mother relented. "We'll try him a whole year."

"But, Mom, I want him to be with us always. He's in bad shape . . . one eye, one arm, one leg."

The mother became impatient. "Son, you're too emotional about this. You've been in a war. The boy will be a drag on you."

Suddenly the boy hung up.

The next day the parents received a telegram from the Navy. Their son had leaped to his death from the twelfth floor of a San Diego hotel.

When the boy's body was shipped home the parents found he had one eye, one arm, and one leg.

Don't you think this family wanted to change their responses to their son? They only had one chance, and they blew it. Some teenagers will only give the church one chance. The one universal need every church should fill is love. If people out there see a diverse group who are still united in love, they will stop and take notice. They will want to be a part of a loving community.

A Tale of Two Churches

The Church of Right

Consider two hypothetical churches. Church number one is heavy on doctrine. The people there want to be right, and they want others to know they're right. Attendance is about 200 on Sunday morning, which is where it's been for more than twenty years. On Sunday night it drops to about 110, and on Wednesday night it goes down to about 95. Those who don't make it to every service are regularly scolded in the bulletin and from the pulpit.

Decisions are made with very little communication other than to tell the members what's been decided. The leaders know they are to edify, so they have three regular assemblies each week plus a potluck once a month. They know they should be involved in benevolence, so they keep a clothes room stocked with worn out, old-fashioned clothes no one wanted anyway.

For evangelism, they make it plain to others in the community how distinctive they are in using the Bible. Their advertising tells others why they're wrong, as do most of the sermons in the assembly. Two gospel meetings are held faithfully every year.

Bickering is common, often over minor issues. The members are well-known in the community for their inability to get along.

The Right Church

Now, church number two also emphasizes doctrine, but it is doctrine that grows out of an intimate relationship with God. Attendance on Sunday morning is also about 200, but it's up forty from two years ago. Nearly 175 come back on Sunday evenings, and almost that many on Wednesday night. No one harangues them about going; they just want to be there.

Nearly 90 per cent of the members can tell you how they fit into the work of the church. They feel a part of it, and decision-making involves communication and input. Edifying is done in the assembly with a sense of excitement, and lessons are geared toward becoming more like Jesus. Smaller groups meet through the month to discuss problems and triumphs more personally.

The congregation actively seeks to minister to the community. They buy a pair of jeans for any school child needing them. They regularly sit down with people going through emotional and physical pain. Evangelism for them is a natural part of that kind of serving. Just as they are concerned about the bodies and minds of others, so they care about their souls. They go to people seeking truth together as friends should.

Which one of these churches would you attend? One church attracts people to Christ, and the other distracts from Christ. One fills the community with the fragrance of Christ, and the other reeks with staleness.

Chum and the Individual Christian

We should determine what type of fishermen we will be. Are we going to hope the fish will hop in our basket or will we use our best chum to bring in full nets? If we plan on doing our best, we must first look at the needs. What is the need we could fill? Jesus gave us a perfect illustration of this in John 4. He was talking to a Samaritan woman who came for water. Her basic existence required water, and Jesus turned a simple conversation about H_2O into a life-changing moment. We need to look for needs in our community, and find a way for Christians to fill them.

Second, we need to earn the respect of those around us. We should examine ourselves to make sure our motives are pure and sincere. Our world hates people without integrity. A Christian should try to keep every area of his life in line

96

with God's will. We also need to confess our weaknesses when we fall. The cocky attitude of the guy who walks down the halls at school thinking all the girls are humming "How Great Thou Art" is an attitude that turns people off. Humility and an awareness of our shortcomings are much more likely to gain respect.

Finally, people should see us emphasizing what's really important. Love should be a foundation quality in our lives. We should stress the things Jesus worried about. We should worry more about the poor and oppressed. We should pay more attention to those who are spiritually sick. Christ didn't waste his time on trivial issues. He came to help people, and we must carry his message to a lost world.

God takes us out in the boat. He grinds us up and throws us back into the water as chum. When people are around us, is the aroma of Christ filling the room? Let's bring the freshness of Christ into our world again.

THOUGHT QUESTIONS FOR CHAPTER 8

1. What needs do you see in your friends or community? Is the church trying to fill these needs?
2. In the description of two chum churches, what made church #2 so much different?
3. What did Jim Woodroof mean in the following statement?
"The crucified Savior can be communicated best through the life of a crucified servant."
4. Examine the conversation between the Samaritan woman and Jesus in John 4. How did he turn it into a spiritual conversation?

ACTIVITY

Select a volunteer to leave the room while you give the rest of your group instructions.
1. Form a circle by interlocking arms.
2. No matter what the leader says, do not let the volunteer into the circle.
3. Begin singing "A Common Love" and call the volunteer back.
4. The leader should be in the center of the circle and begin encouraging the volunteer to join the circle. Make statements like:
    a. We really need you. We love you!
    b. Try another part of the circle if they won't let you in.
    c. It is so neat to love each other like we do. We are such a close youth group.
    d. You really need this group. Try harder to get in.
5. Stop the song and ask kids to tell their feelings.
6. Did they feel bad, good, lonely, embarrassed?
7. Notice how many times the volunteer tried to get into the group.
8. Did he or she get through, only to be pushed back out?

CHAPTER 9

Lost Without Your Love

What comes to your mind when you think about mission work? Do you see a couple paddling down a river in the jungles of Africa? If that's your picture, I want you to explore some new thoughts on God's plan for saving the world.

Our congregations have made us feel comfortable by sending missionaries all over the world. We sometimes feel like we have done our duty by dropping some money in a collection plate. People actually think Matthew 28:19 says, "Therefore, give and let your missionaries make disciples of all nations." Some people will naturally be better at reaching the lost, but telling others about Jesus is not something you delegate. Every Christian has a responsibility to spread the word.

A humorous, convicting story by Max Lucado underscores our responsibility to shine in a dark world:

A few nights ago a peculiar thing happened.

An electrical storm caused a blackout in our neighborhood. When the lights went out, I felt my way through the darkness into the storage closet where we keep the candles for nights like this. Through the glow of a lit match I looked up on the shelf where the candles were stored. There they were, already positioned in their stands, melted to various degrees by previous missions. I took my match and lit four of them.

How they illuminated the storage room! What had been a veil of blackness suddenly radiated with soft, golden light! I could see the freezer I had just bumped with my knee. And I could see my tools that needed to be straightened.

"How great it is to have light!" I said out loud, and then spoke to the candles. "If you do such a good job here in the storage closet, just wait till I get you out where you're really needed! I'll put one of you on the table so we can eat. I'll put one of you on my desk so I can read. I'll give one of you to Denalyn so she can cross-stitch. And I'll set you," I took down the largest one, "in the living room where you can light up the whole area." (I felt a bit foolish talking to candles—but what do you do when the lights go out?)

I was turning to leave with the large candle in my hand when I heard a voice, "Now, hold it right there."

I stopped. *Somebody's in here!* I thought. Then I relaxed. *It's just Denalyn, teasing me for talking to the candles.*

"OK, honey, cut the kidding," I said in the semidarkness. No answer. *Hmm, maybe it was the wind.* I took another step.

"Hold it, I said!" There was that voice again. My hands began to sweat.

"Who said that?"

"I did." The voice was near my hand.

"Who are you? What are you?"

"I'm a candle." I looked at the candle I was holding. It was burning a strong, golden flame. It was red and sat on a heavy wooden candle holder that had a firm handle.

I looked around once more to see if the voice could be coming from another source. "There's no one here but you, me, and the rest of us candles," the voice informed me.

I lifted up the candle to take a closer look. You won't believe what I saw. There was a tiny face in the wax. (I told you you wouldn't believe me.) Not just a wax face that someone had carved, but a moving, functioning, fleshlike face full of expression and life.

"Don't take me out of here!"

"What?"

"I said, don't take me out of this room."

"What do you mean? I have to take you out. You're a candle. Your job is to give light. It's dark out there. People are stubbing their toes and walking into walls. You have to come out and light up this place!"

"But you can't take me out. I'm not ready," the candle explained with pleading eyes. "I need more preparation."

I couldn't believe my ears. "More preparation?"

"Yeah, I've decided I need to research this job of light-giving so I won't go out and make a bunch of mistakes. You'd be surprised how distorted the glow of an untrained candle can be. So I'm doing some studying. I just finished a book on wind resistance. I'm in the middle of a great series of tapes on wick build-up and conservation—and I'm reading the new bestseller on flame display. Have you heard of it?"

"No," I answered.

"You might like it. It's called *Waxing Eloquently.*"

"That really sounds inter—" I caught myself. *What am I doing? I'm in here conversing with a candle while my wife and daughters are out there in the darkness!*

"All right then," I said. "You're not the only candle on the shelf. I'll blow you out and take the others!"

But just as I got my cheeks full of air, I heard other voices.

"We aren't going either!"

It was a conspiracy. I turned around and looked at the three other candles; each with flames dancing above a miniature face.

I was beyond feeling awkward about talking to candles. I was getting miffed.

"You are candles and your job is to light dark places!"

"Well, that may be what you think," said the candle on the far left—a long, thin fellow with a goatee and a British accent. "*You* may think we have to go, but I'm busy."

"Busy?"

"Yes, I'm meditating."

"What? A candle that meditates?"

"Yes. I'm meditating on the importance of light. It's really enlightening."

I decided to reason with them. "Listen, I appreciate what you guys are doing. I'm all for meditation time. And everyone needs to study and research; but for goodness' sake, you guys have been in here for weeks! Haven't you had enough time to get your wick on straight?"

"And you other two," I asked, "are you going to stay in here as well?"

A short, fat, purple candle with plump cheeks that reminded me of Santa Claus spoke up. "I'm waiting to get my life together. I'm not stable enough. I lose my temper easily. I guess you could say that I'm a hothead."

The last candle had a female voice, very pleasant to the ear. "I'd like to help," she explained, "but lighting the darkness is not my gift."

All this was sounding too familiar. "Not your gift? What do you mean?"

"Well, I'm a singer. I sing to other candles to encourage them to burn more brightly." Without asking my permission, she began a rendition of "This Little Light of Mine." (I have to admit, she had a good voice.)

The other three joined in, filling the storage room with singing.

"Hey," I shouted above the music, "I don't mind if you sing while you work! In fact, we could use a little music out there!"

They didn't hear me. They were singing too loudly. I yelled louder.

"Come on, you guys. There's plenty of time for this later. We've got a crisis on our hands."

They wouldn't stop. I put the big candle on the shelf and took a step back and considered the absurdity of it all. Four perfectly healthy candles singing to each other about light but refusing to come out of the closet. I had all I could take. One by one I blew them out. They kept singing to the end. The last one to flicker was the female. I snuffed her out right in the "puff" part of "Won't let Satan puff me out."

I stuck my hands in my pocket and walked back out in the darkness. I bumped my knee on the same freezer. Then I bumped into my wife.

"Where are the candles?" she asked.

"They don't . . . they won't work. Where did you buy those candles anyway?"

"Oh, they're church candles. Remember the church that closed down across town? I bought them there."

I understood.[1]

Jesus is counting on you and me to shine in this world. The crisis is that our churches have become safe shelters where we can take refuge three times a week. We run from our saintly shelters to our homes for a meal with our Christian friends to avoid contamination. We stay away from the non-Christians, and we don't dare bring them into our sanitary shelters. We scurry like little mice from one Christian environment to another, hoping we won't be caught talking to an outsider. We love it once we are inside the walls of safety, and one man begins the pep rally for our team. He talks about how great we are and how badly we need to beat the other side. The problem is that no one wants to step onto the field of life. We would prefer to have pep rallies every week and just talk about the game. A major goal of many churches has been to get the people to fill the

---

[1]From Max Lucado, *God Came Near* (Portland: Multnomah Press, 1987) pp. 113-17. Used by permission.

pews, but I think God's major goal is to get those people out of the pews—out where they can change the world. As John Wesley said, nothing is more unchristian than a solitary Christian. Our detachment from the world's values must be matched by our commitment to its needy people.

Some think that participating once a year on campaigns fulfills their evangelism responsibilities. Campaigns are an opportunity to grow spiritually, to encourage a weak church and to proclaim Christ in a community that doesn't know him. The problem is that evangelism shouldn't stop when you go back home. Teenagers can talk to strangers in the Northeast, but they often freeze when their best friend at home asks about church. The best method of evangelism is

still through a long-term relationship. One trusted friend sharing the Good News with another friend.

Some have even turned evangelism into a spiritual manhunt. The non-Christian prey is identified, and the God-Squad is mobilized. We need to quit seeing people as projects. Evangelism is not something you do to someone. It is communicating a message. In 2 Corinthians 5:20, we are called Christ's ambassadors. We represent the King of Kings.

Some people appeal to the verse that says, "Abstain from all appearance of evil" (1 Thessalonians 5:22, KJV) as a basis for staying away from non-Christians. Some have taken it to mean that we should stay away not only from evil but from everything that looks like evil to anyone else. You can see how it would cut down on ministry, however, if you could never be in a situation someone might interpret as shady. It would cut out a lot of the work of Jesus, for example.

But note other translations of the verse. The Revised Standard Version reads: "Abstain from every form of evil." The New International Version says, "Avoid every kind of evil." Not every appearance of evil, everything that might look evil, but every *form* of evil. Not, "Stay away from everything that somebody might raise an eyebrow about," but "run from things that bring temptation close to your heart."

Loving the Lost

Jesus spent his time in the world. His time was very limited so he had to set some priorities. He chose a band of men to follow him closely who definitely did not have it all together spiritually. But they were devoted! These men received a majority of his time because of their great mission after he would leave the earth.

Now, who did he spend time with besides the apostles? He was found among tax collectors and prostitutes. Matthew 11:19 says he was a *friend* of sinners. He not only ate with them, but he was their friend.

He received quite a few critical comments, and he raised a number of eyebrows. He didn't care what others thought. His priority was to call the spiritually sick, not the healthy. (See his illustration of the sick who need a doctor in Matthew 9:12 and 13.)

When a doctor's beeper goes off, it tells us that a physician is needed because somebody is sick. It doesn't go off every time someone feels well. The physician is for those who are ill.

That's what Jesus was saying. "I'm here for those who are ill. The ones who think they have it all together spiritually I cannot minister to, so I am here for tax collectors and sinners—those broken souls who want my help." Aren't you thankful that he is!

The problem the Pharisees had was isolation. There is a classic story in Luke 7:36-50 that shows the Pharisees' mindset. A sinful woman brings Jesus an expensive jar of perfume. She begins to weep because her heart is heavy with sin. She anoints him with oil, then dries his feet with her own hair and kisses them. The Pharisees watch all this happen, and they are having a fit. Finally, the host says to himself, "If this man were a prophet, he would know who is touching him and what kind of woman she is—that she is a *sinner!*" The host considered her not good enough to be in their exclusive religious club because she was a sinner.

It is interesting to me how the room was filled with religious people, yet she went straight to Jesus with her broken heart. The Great Physician went to work, and Jesus forgave her sins and healed her guilt.

We need to be a friend to sinners just like Jesus. Jesus was a teacher, but he was a friend first. He ministered to the people who just casually entered his life. He filled their needs and moved on.

As Rebecca Pippert wrote in her book *Out of the Salt Shaker*:

I am saying that by far the most effective, the most costly, and even perhaps the most biblical kind of evangelism is found in the person or groups who look at the people around them, those with whom their own life naturally intersects and then begin to cultivate friendships and to love them.

Let's look at some principles Jesus used to establish his relationships with people.

1. *Find some common interests.* In Matthew 9, Jesus was eating with Matthew, building a bridge by doing something together. We could do that, couldn't we? Most of us eat regularly. The people around us eat regularly. One way to establish a relationship is to do things together. We can expand the list to include racquetball, golf, tennis, band, fishing, hunting, sewing, movies and concerts, service clubs, hiking, scouting, jogging, and so on.

2. *Practice hospitality.* Jesus couldn't invite people to his house because for most of his life he had no place to lay his head. He was a traveling preacher. But still he knew the comfort of being in a home. So he went to Matthew's house, and suddenly the barriers were laid down at the door. What did he say to Zacchaeus when he met him? "Zacchaeus, I'm going to your house today." When we see a spark of interest, we need to create a situation where we can share.

3. *See the lostness of the people.* Jesus came to save the lost. His heart went out to the poor, the lonely, the fearful, and the suffering, but he would do anything to bring one more person into heaven. A teacher recently told a group of teens he had lost a $100.00 bill. They all blinked their eyes in disbelief, but no one moved. The teacher then said, "Anyone who finds it will get to keep it." The teens went crazy searching for that money. The teacher stopped them after thirty seconds. He then asked the class, "Would you react in the same energetic way if I gave you

a teenager's name that was lost? Would you jump up immediately and go look for him? How much is a soul worth today? $100? $200?" I think sometimes we have lost our belief that anyone is really lost. You may think heaven and hell are just a fantasy someone made up to be funny. God promises you they are realities!

There is a great drama skit that is very powerful. It shows a judgment day scene with one young Christian man standing over to one side. His best friend comes before God and hears God say, "Depart from me." The friend looks at his Christian friend and screams, "Why didn't you tell me? I thought you cared about me." A girl he sat next to in biology class walks up to God next and hears, "Depart from me." She turns to the Christian boy and says, "How could you let this happen to me? Why didn't you tell me about Jesus? I thought you loved me." Do you get the picture? The world is lost unless you love them enough to share Jesus.

We need to see people around us in a different way. We usually notice them for their looks and talents, but wee need to see deeper than the surface. We need to see the hearts of people who don't know Jesus. It isn't natural to look at people in this way, but we must see our world through the loving eyes of Jesus. When we see and love as Jesus did, we will have a dramatic impact on our world.

THOUGHT QUESTIONS FOR CHAPTER 9

1. Do you think Christians ever get selective about who should hear about Jesus? WHY?
2. Do you feel any responsibility to spread the word about Jesus? Why or why not?
3. Should a Christian teen go into a bar to associate with a sinner? What are some of the dangers of that situation?
4. How did Jesus handle criticism from the Pharisees for hanging out with known sinners?
5. If Jesus came to your school cafeteria, which group of people do you think he would go visit with first?
6. If we are supposed to do the things Jesus would do, what changes should be made in our attitudes and behavior?

ACTIVITY

1. Break the teens into small groups of 8-10.
2. Design a simulation survival group.
   A sample is listed below:
   a. A newly married Christian couple
   b. A homosexual male—age 47
   c. A woman atheist—age 24
   d. A black bar owner—age 35
   e. A boy currently dying of cancer—age 15
   f. A recovering alcoholic woman who just began attending church again—age 32
   g. Woman (f)'s baby—age 1
3. Your small group of teens must decide four people who will die and four people who will live.

4. The purpose of the exercise is to see how your group views the lost and the saved.
5. The question to ask after your groups make their decisions is, Who would Jesus choose?

CHAPTER 10

The Modern Jesus

Several years ago, Diane and I visited a small congregation. Before we walked in, someone warned me to hide my Bible because it wasn't a King James Version. I tried to explain that it was my Greek Bible, but she said, "They think all those translations are liberal." So, I tucked my Greek Bible under my coat and went in the building.

The preacher covered every sin in the Bible plus a few extras. The main point, though, was mixed swimming. For about thirty minutes we heard a fierce attack on mixed swimming. The best I could tell, Diane and I were the only ones in the audience under the age of 80, and we were visitors. I had the feeling the message was a bit irrelevant, given the audience.

Several years ago, a missionary from Kenya spoke for chapel at Harding Graduate School. "Don't worship your ancestors," he warned us. "Don't worship your ancestors. . . ." I've never been tempted to do that. I honor those who have come before me, but ancestral worship is not one of my danger areas.

Then he paused and said, "You know, I'm not really speaking to you very well, am I?" We were all thinking, *No, not at all.* He said, "That's what I have to preach in Kenya. My message must begin with ancestral worship. If I'm ever going to reach out to those people I must begin where they are and then reach down into their ultimate needs. And yet, I wonder how many of you speak to people in irrelevant ways as well, talking about things they don't care about, speaking about items that don't concern them."

The point is well taken. If we're going to be the aroma of Christ in the world, we must be relevant. We must communicate a message that makes sense.

We need an effective communication strategy for the gospel of Christ. Let's consider how we should share our faith.

1. *Begin With Felt Needs.* Our main task in reaching lost people is to identify their specific needs. We all have needs, but they are different for each individual. This makes it impossible to write down a set formula on how to share Jesus. It would be great to use a memorized speech with each

person, but look at how Jesus approached people in the gospels. Each person was handled in a different way depending on his or her need. He gave knowledge to those seeking more truth. He healed those who came with medical problems before he attempted to give them a theological lesson on his power. Jesus listened intently to each person until he found the need. He then used that need to open the door of communication.

If we begin telling everyone a message without considering his need, the message may be filtered out. Everyone has a filter. It sorts through all the messages that the media and others bombard us with. Let me show you how a filter works. Anyone who has flown on an airplane will know exactly what I am talking about.

I have ridden on a plane many times during my lifetime. At the beginning of each flight, a stewardess launches into a memorized flight lecture concerning the oxygen masks, seat belts, and emergency exits. Do you listen? Does anyone listen? Usually not! It never gets through the filter because we've heard it before. We know about the masks falling from the ceiling and the seat bottom being a flotation device.

Another example of our filter at work is when the broadcasters of a ball game begin their warning about rebroadcasting the game without the "expressed written consent" of the commissioner. Rarely do we actually *hear* that warning because we've heard it too many times. Instead, we filter it out.

There are people around you who have heard about Jesus from a variety of sources. If you started telling them about God, the filter would probably stop the message from getting to their heart. We need to find ways to work around those filters, and we can by finding a need that will open the door to their minds and their hearts.

Some people don't care about the gospel. We've said for a long time that "Everybody's just waiting to hear the Good News of Christ." That's just not true. Studies show that about sixty per cent of all non-Christians are very satisfied with their lives. They aren't sitting around just hoping someone will ask them to a Bible study. Their lives are so full of other temporary thrills that they don't have room for God in their schedules.

Our opportunity to break through with the gospel message will usually begin with basic Christian service: going out of our way to befriend someone lonely at school, listening (without offering endless advice!) to someone who just experienced the break-up of a dating relationship, accepting the frightened fourteen-year-old who just learned she's pregnant.

Where are people right now? What about the young couple who just lost their one-year-old son to a disease? What could we do for the girl whose parents just filed for divorce? How would you show love to the girl who wears the same three outfits to school each week because her dad is unemployed?

Let's see how Jesus did it. He met a blind man (John 9). What did he do? He gave him sight. What did he do then? Did he preach the message to him? No, he left. He met the man where he was and then went on his way. That should tell us that we can give a cup of water in Jesus' name without sticking a gospel tract in it.

The world can distinguish between real love and love with strings attached. We must look for and be sensitive to the needs of others, but we must also keep our motivation pure. Jesus wants us to give because we love others, but it is so easy to demand something in return. When I feed you in order to baptize you, I may be trying to manipulate you. If we can relieve some anxiety, sit quietly with a grief-stricken widow, buy clothes for the poor, we make the world a better place in which to live. We also let people get a small taste of the love Jesus offers.

2. *Change the Words, But Not the Message.* How many books remain relevant 2000 years after they were written? The Bible can be applied to our lives even today, but we must show our world how it relates to each unique culture.

Jesus spoke to thousands of people who had heard everything about religion. They had their filters ready anytime someone brought up a religious topic. He found that using parables was an effective way to teach these particular people. He'd sneak up behind them with a story, and by the end they had learned some great lessons. The parable of the Good Samaritan is a good example.

The people first heard that a Samaritan helped the injured man. This would catch a Jew's attention quickly. It doesn't strike you as strongly because you've heard it before. What if I told you a story about the Good Communist who helped a dying U.S. diplomat? Get the idea? Jesus used modern day examples for his era—we need to do the same thing.

Some of the greatest teachers I know present old lessons in new and creative ways. One teacher held out a closed fist. He told his class there was money in his closed hand, and he offered it to anyone who had enough faith in him to come get the money. At first no one moved, but finally one boy moved to the front and took the money. He got the kids' attention, but he also made Hebrews 11:1 a verse to remember. Faith in things not seen became crystal clear to a roomful of kids that day!

Paul would never change his Christian morals or message, but he would try to identify with his audience. Paul described this ministry style in 1 Corinthians 9:19-23. When he preached to the Jews, he became Jewish. He went to the temple and offered a sacrifice, knowing that it didn't bring forgiveness, but dedicating it to the glory of God (Acts 21). When he was with Gentiles, he became like a Gentile. He honored their customs and respected their viewpoint. Here's the reason: "I have become all things to all men so that by all possible means I might save some" (1 Corinthians 9:22). Paul identified with his audience.

3. *Point to the One Who Fulfills Our Ultimate Needs.* We must begin where people are, and we cannot manipulate them in order to reach a certain point. We shared our unconditional love in order for them to see what Jesus' love is like. When our words and lifestyle reflect Jesus our friends

should understand his teachings better. They understand why he served others when we serve others. They understand how Jesus loved his enemies when they see us love our enemies. All the lessons *about* Jesus won't teach them nearly as much as a life dedicated to living *like* him will teach.

We should discuss some basic issues that are central to the Christian life. We love to talk about specific issues that are highly controversial, but that is not what we need to bombard a non-Christian with. Here are a few things we need to discuss with them:

● THE BIBLE. This is God's message to us. It is a trustworthy source for learning about the work of God.

● SIN IS UNIVERSAL. Sin separates all men from God (Romans 3:23). The punishment for sin is death, and someone must pay the price (Romans 6:23).

● JESUS. He is the one who paid the price so that we can go to heaven. He died for us, and we should dedicate our lives to him. His love for us should motivate us toward service to him.

● DYING TO SELF (Galatians 2:20). When we are baptized into Christ, we die. All our desires and actions should reflect Christ. Our decisions should not be made for our own best interests. We should do what Jesus would do in that particular situation.

● THE CHURCH. This is the family God raised up to change the world. It is a body of believers who live in praise to God, who encourage the spiritually weak, who carry the burdens of weary strugglers.

● FAITH (Hebrews 11). Faith is belief that moves you into acts of obedience. Mere "belief" is not enough. Satan believes in the existence of God, but he chooses not to serve him.

Our biggest challenge is to keep the message of Christ clear and simple. We pride ourselves on sharing deep thoughts and finding new ideas in the Bible. A two-year-old girl brought everything into focus for one church recently. The communion service was solemn and reverent. One of the deacons led a beautiful prayer about Jesus. Heads were bowed for individual meditation, but a blonde-haired two-year-old began to sing "Jesus Loves Me." The problem was that her singing was loud enough for several hundred people to hear. The parents were noticeably embarrassed, and a few people looked disturbed. Her parents tried to lower her volume, but the little girl only sang louder. She finished the song just as the communion service finished. It was all perfect. A communion service reflecting on Jesus' death. A small innocent voice singing "Jesus Loves Me," and a church focusing on the central message of Jesus through the pure heart of the little girl. Isn't that what it's all about?

THOUGHT QUESTIONS FOR CHAPTER 10

1. Do we communicate Jesus effectively by standing in front of a TV camera wearing a multi-colored wig and wearing a shirt with John 3:16 on it?
2. What are the best ways to get your friends involved in a spiritual conversation?
3. Can we just live Christian lives or do we have a responsibility to *tell* our friends about Jesus?
4. What filters do we have to work through in sharing Jesus today?

ACTIVITY

Choose any Bible story to create a modern day parable. Use modern technology and your own creativity to illustrate a principle of God's Word.

CHAPTER 11

Not Built for Guilt

The cross and resurrection of Jesus address the three most haunting problems of our age: guilt (a problem with the past), meaninglessness (a problem with the present), and hopelessness (a problem with the future). This chapter will look at the problems our past can cause in our lives.

Guilt is something everyone has felt. It may be extremely intense, or it may be a mild, uncomfortable feeling. We sometimes call it a conscience. One teenager described his conscience as what his mother would say if she knew what he had done! This feeling was put there by God to make us aware that sin is in our lives. Sin separates us from God, and the separation produces guilt.

God's plan was simple. We are human so we will sin, yet he hoped we wouldn't be comfortable living in sin. He gave his Son to pay our debt to sin and guilt (Romans 3:23, 6:23). Yet, some people still remain chained to sin.

Thomas Costain wrote a history book called *The Three Edwards*, describing the life of Raynald III, a 14th Century Duke of what is now Belgium. Grossly overweight, he was commonly called, Crassus, which means "fat."

After a heated quarrel, Raynald's younger brother, Edward, led a revolt against him. Edward captured Raynald, but did not kill him. Instead he built a room around Raynald in his castle and promised him he could have his property and his kingdom back as soon as he was able to leave the room.

This would not have been difficult for most people since the room had several windows and a door of near normal size which were not barred or locked. The problem was Raynald's size. To have his freedom he needed only to lose weight. But Edward knew his older brother, and each day he sent a variety of delicious foods. Instead of dieting his way out of prison, Raynald grew larger and larger.

When Duke Edward was accused of unusual cruelty, he had a ready answer: "My brother is not a prisoner. He may leave when he so wills."

Raynald stayed in that same room for ten years, and wasn't released until after Edward died in battle. By then his health was so ruined that he died within a year . . . a prisoner of his own appetite.

In a similar way, we sometimes imprison ourselves to sin. God never intended for us to be slaves to sin. He made us so that we could be sons and daughters of hope. God didn't design our hearts to carry the weight of sin. He didn't plan for us to carry a guilty conscience around for life. We weren't built to carry guilt. Guilt may be a signal that our lives aren't right with God, but God wants us to make a change and unload the guilt.

The world might tell you to deny your guilt feelings. Many psychologists believe you should do whatever you would like; they want you to think there are no absolutes in life. The problem is there *are* absolutes! Common sense, not just the Bible, tells us murder is wrong. There is no way to justify killing someone because you feel like it. Your conscience will tell you something is not quite right.

Let's look at three ways the world has tried to handle guilt:
1. *Denial.* This doesn't help very much because you still

have the problem of the conscience. You may appear very calm to your peers, but your insides keep churning.

2. *Concealment.* I love the story of Achan in Joshua 7. He had ripped off some things at Jericho that he shouldn't have taken. He thought he could get away with it, but the Israelites lost the next battle at Ai. The Lord guaranteed no victories would come until Achan uncovered his sin. King David also tried to conceal his immoral relationship with Bathsheba. He got the word she was pregnant, so he used

his power as king to cover his sin. Neither of these guys came up with the right solution, though. Until their sins were uncovered, they lived in fear.

3. *Working to make up for your sin.* Some may think, "If I work harder and do more, I can get rid of this nagging guilt. I'm going to read my Bible more. I'm going to pray more. I'll go to every devotional. I've got to do everything possible to get rid of this guilt."

Paul gave the only answer for guilt in his first letter to the Corinthians. He began, "For I am the least of the apostles and do not even deserve to be called an apostle, because I persecuted the church of God" (1 Corinthians 15:9). Paul looked to the past and said, "I did some things wrong. I blew it! This beautiful church of God is the very church I was out to persecute!" Did he say it with self-condemnation? No. Did he say it with guilt? No. Paul had experienced God's forgiveness.

We can live with a knowledge of the past and yet not be bound to the guilt of forgiven sins. We can't deny it ever happened, and we can't erase the memory from our minds. Let's look at how we can really deal with our guilt. Here'a two-step approach:

1. Accept the gift of grace. Too often we feel that we got ourselves into the mess, and *we* have to get ourselves out of it. But Paul said, "That's not the way it works. I persecuted my church, but God's grace reached down to me. Look how it has changed my life."

God has to take the initiative, and he did. Isaiah said concerning the servant of God:

Surely he took up our infirmities and carried our sorrows, yet we considered him stricken by God, smitten by him, and afflicted. But he was pierced for our transgressions, he was crushed for our iniquities; the punishment that brought us peace was upon him, and by his wounds we are healed. We all, like sheep, have gone astray, each of us has turned to his own way; and the Lord has laid on him the iniquity of us all (Isaiah 53:4-6).

That's where the cross comes in. God sent his Son. He died on the cross, carrying our sin, and our guilt.

Just before Christmas, 1988 a Pan Am flight crashed in Scotland. It had originated in Frankfurt and had stopped in London before heading for the United States. A couple of days after the fatal crash a wreath showed up at the scene of the wreck. It had a note from a lady who had gotten off the plane in London: "To the little girl in the red dress who made my trip from Frankfurt to London so much fun. You didn't deserve this."

That could be said of Jesus at the cross: he didn't deserve it. He carried our sin and guilt. So our salvation is not by being morally perfect; it's not by our own righteousness; it's by the righteousness of *Christ* that God says, "All right. By your faith when you come into Christ in baptism, I'm going to declare you righteous." Then you are at one with God, and *all* your sins are washed away.

2. Accept the life of grace. "His grace to me was not without effect. No, I worked harder than all of them—yet now I, but the grace of God that was with me" (1 Corinthians 15:10b).

The legalistic approach to the law says we need to perform so we can be accepted. Grace says we are accepted, so we're free to follow Christ. Those are two entirely different perspectives. Paul was saying, "I am what I am by grace. I've been accepted by God, and therefore I want to live the grace-filled life. I want to live right and stop doing wrong."

Don't be fooled by your feelings, though. You may not feel forgiven when you first become a Christian. As you get into Christian activities and start doing right, your emotions will eventually come around. They will confirm in your mind what has already happened—God has forgiven you.

Some of the most guilt-ridden, fearful people in the world are in our churches. You can't talk to them about freedom from the past because they haven't experienced it. They sing, "My sin—oh the bliss of this glorious thought—my sin, not in part but the whole, is nailed to the cross and I bear it no more," but many don't believe it. They don't feel like they have heard a real sermon unless they feel guilty. They don't feel the preacher is doing his job if he doesn't stomp on their toes.

It's important to distinguish between two kinds of guilt. One is objective guilt. This is when you have done something against God. It may be mistreating your neighbor, but it is still a sin against God. When you've done something wrong before God, you're guilty whether you feel it or not. Some people can do so many wrong things that it causes their conscience to become calloused. They are able to do horrible things without feeling guilty, even though they are.

The other kind of guilt is subjective guilt. This is when we don't disappoint God really, but we don't measure up to our own expectations. Kids usually get subjective guilt at camp. They know camp has been great. They have prayed all the time and read their Bibles three times a day. The problem is that they don't do that normally. Many kids come to ask for prayers so they can be better. The thing is they were great kids before they ever came to camp. They struggled through a tough school year and resisted Satan, but they still feel guilty.

I think a lot of teens feel guilt because of their picture of

God. Each person views God in a variety of ways, but I have noticed a stereotype that teens often come up with to describe God.

Some people think God is like a policeman. He is always hiding behind something just waiting for you to make a mistake. Just as soon as you commit your sin, God jumps out and shoots you with his .357 Magnum misery gun. He gives you a disease or causes some trouble in your life to teach you a lesson. One young lady told me that she often dreams that Jesus is making her walk a tightrope. He sternly watches as she cries, knowing that if she falls she'll go straight to hell. This young sister in Christ has a wrong view of God!

I think the Bible uses a great analogy throughout its pages. The writers call him Father. Suppose a young person prays at night before he goes to sleep. He is so tired that he falls asleep before he is finished. The next day he feels guilty because he went to sleep on God.

Let's apply the Father image to this same situation. A little girl goes to bed, and she's talking to her father about the day's activities. Her eyes grow heavy as she begins talking about her plans tomorrow. In the middle of a sentence she falls asleep. How does the father react? "I'm not going to be treated that way ever again. That is the last time I'll ever tuck her in bed!" He stomps out of the room slamming the door firmly behind him. Speaking as a dad, that isn't what happens! Fathers understand the struggles of their children, and God is no different. While he is a high and holy God demanding reverence and worship, he is also a loving Father filled with compassion.

Our teaching has sometimes been so negative that we can't enjoy being a Christian. We may have been given an unbalanced view of Christianity. Being a Christian is not just avoiding all the bad activities. It is walking in a loving faith relationship with God.

Where does this self-condemnation come from? Sometimes it comes from our religious background. Whether

people told us so or not, we perceive our religion as saying that we must be exactly like God before we'll ever be accepted. We've got to be perfect. I've heard many teens talk about becoming a Christian, but they want to eliminate all their faults first. They face two major problems, though. First, they will never eliminate *all* their flaws, and they will always be imperfect. Second, they try to get their lives cleaned up without God. They want to do it without the spiritual forces of God.

You may become a Christian, but Satan doesn't quit working on you. He is the one who will try to get you to quit. He will trip you time after time, hoping that you won't have the spiritual strength to get back on your feet. He tries to convince you that God can't possibly love a sinner like you.

The good news is your sins are washed away . . .

"If you walk in the light as he is in the light, the blood of Christ keeps washing away our sins" (1 John 1:7, paraphrased). You're not in Christ at 10 o'clock and out of him at 10:30, back in him at 11:00, and out again at 11:30. *You stay there.* You may do something wrong, but you're still guiltless before God because you've been accepted. He is your full-time Lord. He is always there for you, and he will always love you. He asks you to make the same commitment to him.

Another reason teens carry guilt is the hidden "unforgivable sin." Some kids believe they committed a sin so horrible that God couldn't possibly forgive them. This secret is usually tucked away in the back of a young person's heart, and it continues to haunt him the rest of his life.

I love the story of Joseph's brothers selling him because it shows "how guilt is carried for a lifetime." We pick up on the story as the brothers travel to Egypt looking for food. Many years have gone by since they sold Joseph. They walk into Joseph's royal chamber not recognizing the older Joseph, but he certainly knows them. Joseph threw all the brothers into prison for a few days to let them experience what he had been through. In Genesis 42:21, the brothers are all discussing their misfortune. Notice what hidden events pop into their guilty minds first. They said to one another, "Surely we are being punished because of our brother (Joseph). We saw how distressed he was when he pleaded with us for his life, but we would not listen, and that's why this distress has come upon us." See how their guilt continued to haunt them?

But Jesus died for all our sins. No sin you've committed is too great for him to forgive you. We must find a way to let go of our guilt, or it will destroy us. James 5:16 commands us to "confess your sins to each other." Why? We need help in dealing with our struggles, and this keeps us from hiding the scars of sin. Have you ever lied about something to your parents? It takes so much energy to keep that secret from your parents. All the facts must remain straight in your mind. Most of the time, you worry about someone telling your parents what really happened. After you handle all of that, you still must wrestle with your conscience.

A young man was struggling with some hard moral decisions. Satan was winning the struggle when he had a dream. He began the dream in a huge body of water. He realized he was half-way between the ocean floor and the surface of the water. He began to feel his lungs aching for oxygen. He tried to tell which way to swim, and began making powerful strokes toward the surface. His lungs began to burn as he kept reaching for that precious air. By now, his body screamed for oxygen to fill his lungs. He reached up with his hand to pull his body to the surface, but when he cupped his hand, he felt sand. He had gone the wrong way. His direction was confused, and he had gone to the bottom. His conscience told him something that night with brutal honesty. He was confused intellectually, and his current direction was not right. No matter how well he fooled everyone else, he couldn't fool himself.

The Bible is filled with stories about people who handled guilt the wrong way, as well as many who handled it right. Saul handled his guilt by becoming bitter and jealous. David did some horrible things, but he turned to God. Judas betrayed the Son of God. Judas thought he couldn't be forgiven, and he became so depressed that he killed himself. Paul persecuted the same church he would one day help, but Paul knew he wasn't built to carry guilt. Paul became a new man because of the total forgiveness he received.

I believe in change. A person can hand over a garbage dumpster full of guilt and be cleansed by the blood of Christ FOREVER.

THOUGHT QUESTIONS FOR CHAPTER 11

1. When you sin, how do you handle it?
   A. Denial—It wasn't a sin
   B. Conceal it—Hide it from others
   C. Rationalize—It wasn't my fault
   D. Do lots of good deeds to make up for it.
2. Why is it so hard to confess our sins to each other in the church?
3. How could the church or your youth group improve openness about sharing struggles?
4. Does God *only* forgive the sins we mention in prayers?
5. Read Luke 6:37. How does your attitude of forgiveness affect God's attitude toward your forgiveness?

ACTIVITY

Gather the following items to represent the designated events:

A. Car fender or car tire—accident you had that no one knows about

B. Small ladder—sneaking out of your house at night

C. Toilet paper—wrapped your Youth Minister's house (the unforgivable sin)

D. Sledgehammer or crowbar—breaking into a house to steal things

E. Large brick—vandalism

F. Baseball bat—fighting

G. Sword—stabbing others in the back or Megaphone—gossip

H. Etc. (Think up more using your own creativity.)

Procedure:

1. Hide the items, if possible, from the group.

2. Pick one strong volunteer who will carry these items of guilt for you.

3. Bring out the items one at a time, telling what sin each symbolizes.

4. Don't let your volunteer put anything down once you hand it to him. He/She must hold onto it.

5. Keep piling it on until you run out of objects, or your volunteer gets tired. This illustrates how we aren't built to carry a heavy load of guilt.

6. Let the volunteer put down the items carefully, and let him read 1 John 1:7.

7. Move into the discussion questions using the props for illustrations.

CONCEALMENT—Roleplay a teen carrying a car bumper and trying to hide it from his friends.

CHAPTER 12

An End to Trivial Pursuits

Why Are We Here?

Woody Allen once remarked: "More than any other time in history, mankind faces a crossroads: One path leads to despair and utter hopelessness. The other to total extinction. Let us pray we have the wisdom to choose correctly."

Ouch! I don't care much for that choice. But he seems to have captured the despair which many teenagers face.

Ernest Hemingway's *The Old Man and the Sea* is a parable for modern man. The old man believed he would catch a blue marlin that would exceed all other fish ever caught. Every day he journeyed out in his beat-up old boat looking for that one great marlin. Every day he failed. Finally, he latched onto that blue marlin of his dreams. He pulled it up next to the boat. He didn't have modern equipment to bring it into the boat, so he left it in the water and began dragging it back to the coast. As he neared the coastal waters, a shark attacked the marlin and tore it to shreds. When he returned to the shore the greatest catch of his life was now nothing but a few shreds of torn fish.

That story seems to represent the futility Hemingway battled. We go out every day looking for something special. We may think we've found it, but in the moment of crisis, we find it was all an illusion. There is no purpose for our boats going out. The end of Hemingway's life was consistent with his viewpoint in this story, since he ended his life in suicide.

I don't think Ernest Hemingway was the only person who discovered he had no direction in life. A teacher in a church Bible class recently asked a roomful of teenagers for their purpose in life. After an uncomfortable length of silence, one student said, "I don't know why we are here. I wish someone could tell me." I think he spoke for a lot of teenagers who are confused about their role in this world.

Tom Peters, in the first of his two books on excellence, *In Search of Excellence*, quoted a psychologist named Ernest Becker who said, "Society . . . is a vehicle for earthly heroism. . . . It is the burning desire for the creature to count. . . . What man really fears is not so much extinction, but extinction without doing something significant."

The powerful thoughts of Harold Kushner (*When All You've Ever Wanted Isn't Enough*) point out the same fear: "I am convinced that it is not the fear of death, of our lives ending, that haunts our sleep so much as the fear that our lives will not have mattered, that as far as the world is concerned we might as well never have lived. What we miss in our lives, no matter how much we have, is that sense of meaning."

Looking for Meaning

The major problem in our society is that people are looking for meaning in the wrong places. The book of Ecclesiastes begins, "I've tried everything in life. I've seen it all, done it all, and it is all vanity. It won't bring you real happiness or meaning."

Some people have tried to find meaning in money or possessions. Life is filled with things that we really believe will make us happy. Remember as a child the red bike with training wheels that looked so good? You thought that would bring happiness, and your parents bought it for you. Everything was great until you saw a 10-speed bike. You just knew that would make you happy, so you bought it. The bike was okay, but now you have a driver's license. It's hard to pick up a date on a bike, so you thought a car would bring you the ultimate thrill. Your dad found a nice used VW for a few hundred dollars. Can you guess the next want? The VW is old and doesn't run well. You would be happy if you could just drive a 280Z turbo with power windows, power locks, and sun roof. If you could just have the ultimate car you would be happy! Get the idea? It's an endless cycle.

Ecclesiastes warns that money is not going to bring you happiness or meaning. However, the problem with many of us is that we are *always* willing to give money one more chance to make us happy.

Others try sexual activity—the Animal House approach to life. One spokesman for this lifestyle is Gene Simmons from the group "KISS." He had this to say, "My lifestyle is absolutely promiscuous. I don't want to get married or have kids. I want to have as many girls as I can before the ground claims me, and that's what makes me happy." He went on to say that his accomplishments include "increasing the population of the United States noticeably, and waking up in bed with a lot of girls whose names I cannot remember."

Maybe popularity is your goal. Everybody would love to be the school leader. The problem is that popularity is so fleeting. Popularity is something that is given to you by other people. As long as you dress the right way and say the right words, you will be popular. Can you see the trap yet? If you *don't* conform to the group's expectations, you will fail in popularity. There will usually be someone ready to take your place.

At some point in your life, you will have to quit listening to everyone else and decide what *you* think is really important. The media will try to sell you some ideas and even your friends may give you some advice, but the buck stops with you.

There are two specific times when this issue seems to surface: when a person gets out of high school and at middle age. Some young people won't bother to ask what is important in life. They'll take a class because they've got to take it to graduate, and they want to graduate because they've got to graduate to get a job, and they want a job because you've got to have a job to live. They want a job to make the money to buy their things. They want bigger houses to store more things, but their lack of a meaningful direction will only cause unhappiness.

At middle age, people who take this approach to life go through a mid-life crisis. They realize they have invested their time and energies in things that really aren't important to them. They are secure in careers, and they find that it isn't easy to make a change. Their lives have become a trap, and it's too late to start all over again.

Who's in Control Here?

The New Testament speaks of new life and becoming a new creature. When you truly commit your life to something or someone, it will cause some changes.

As a little girl, Mary Lou Retton committed her life to a coach named Bela Karoyli. She made a decision to totally commit her life to becoming an Olympic champion. She left her home and moved to Houston, Texas. She went to school, but after school her time was spent in a sweaty gym. Her diet did not include pizza and soft drinks. She had a strict diet of healthy food and, along with the diet, a rigid curfew. She went through set workout routines each day for years. All the work pointed to that magic moment in 1984. She stood at the end of the long runway. The world watched as she prepared to make her final jump of the Olympics. The gold medal would be hers with a perfect vault. She came down the runway pumping those arms and legs with increasing speed. She hit the ramp and the vault in beautiful style. Her body twisted into position for a perfect landing.

She flashed that beautiful smile to the cameras as the crowd held its breath. All eyes riveted to a blank scoreboard on the floor. Time stood still until the number 10.0 came to the screen.

Every one of you would have traded places with her as she picked up the gold medal, but would you have been committed to the changes that Coach Karoyli demanded? Her coach didn't just give suggestions, he gave commands. Will you give God that much control of your life?

If our goal is to be with God someday, we must commit our lives to him completely. Jesus is such a great example of one who came not to do his will, but the will of God (John 6:38). His life shows us true commitment. We can see it when he was thrown into a garden and came face to face with the shadow of a cross. He struggled, but ultimately he said, "Not my will but thine be done." He was committed to that meaning for his life. When they put him on a cross, he forgave those who persecuted him, in spite of how he felt, because he wanted to do the will of the Father.

Suffering in Life

Paul was a man who gave God control of his life. Paul's words in the New Testament show two things: the reason he didn't mind suffering for a good cause, and the glorious hope he had to be with God someday.

God didn't promise us that a life with meaning would be easy. Paul's life is a great example of this fact. Paul was no stranger to suffering (2 Corinthians 11:23-28). Can you match that list? Look at Paul's mindset, though, in 2 Corinthians 4:7-10. Do you see where Paul finds meaning in his present life? Paul devoted himself to spreading the news about Jesus no matter what the cost. He found meaning in all his suffering because his cause was so important. There are just some persecutions that must be endured for the cause of Christ.

Martin Luther King, Jr. was a man who endured many a storm as he pushed for equality of all people. There were many who tried to discourage these blacks, but they would not be stopped. A group of several hundred blacks began a march from Selma, Alabama. They wanted to draw attention to the problem through a peaceful march to Montgomery. They came to the Pettus Bridge in Selma, Alabama, before local authorities stopped the march. The police stood with their night sticks ready; the blacks stopped, not moving forward or backward. The captain of police demanded that they go back before it was too late. The blacks bowed their heads and prayed. The tension between good and evil rose as the silence declared the importance of this moment. The captain finally gave the word for his forces to push them back. A wave of sticks and police dogs chased the crowd, and the streets became bloody in a matter of minutes. The police thought they had won what historians now call "Bloody Sunday." The interesting note is that the TV crews and photographers showed our nation what really happened. The American people saw the brutality and cruelty, and they rose up in anger. This was a turning point for the blacks. Why didn't they turn back before anyone got hurt? Their cause was simply more important than the hurt of broken bones. What they did was not *easy*, but it was *significant*.

During the boycott of Montgomery buses (because blacks were forced to sit in the back of buses), many walked twelve miles to work. One older lady said: "My feets is tired, but my soul is at rest." Those are words of victory—words of direction and purpose.

Meaning will come to our lives when we commit ourselves to the way of the Cross. "If anyone would come after me, he must deny himself and take up his cross daily and follow me" (Luke 9:23). Then, Jesus said, we will truly find our life (v. 24)!

On January 28, 1986, the space shuttle Challenger burst into a fiery ball, killing all seven crew members. One of those killed was Christa McAuliffe, a school teacher who was to be the first private citizen to travel through space. In Robert Hohler's biography of her, he says she "had asked nothing more than to be an ordinary person on an extraordinary mission."

That is the opportunity you have! By following Jesus, you can join an incredible, extraordinary mission.

Hope of Heaven

God gives our life meaning, and he also gives us hope. Paul brings this out in 2 Corinthians 5:1-10. The people threatened him with death, but his attitude was, "Don't worry, church. They can kill my temporary body, but they can't touch my home in heaven."

In Charles Colson's book *Loving God*, he tells the story of an Asian hermit who lived in a tiny village. He spent most of his time in prayer, until he thought he heard the voice of God telling him to go to Rome. He went to Rome at the time of a great festival. The little monk followed the crowd down the streets into the Colosseum. He saw the gladiators stand before the emperor and say, "We who are about to die salute you." Then he realized these men were going to fight to the death for the entertainment of the crowd. He cried out, "In the name of Christ, stop!"

As the games began, he pushed his way through the crowd, climbed over the wall, and dropped to the floor of the arena. When the crowd saw this tiny figure rushing to the gladiators and saying, "In the name of Christ, stop!" They thought it was part of the show and began laughing. When they realized it wasn't, the laughter turned to anger. As he was pleading with the gladiators to stop, one of them plunged a sword into his body. He fell to the sand. As he was dying, his last words were, "In the name of Christ, stop!'

Then a strange thing happened. The gladiators stood looking at the tiny figure lying there. A hush fell over the Colosseum. Way up in the upper rows, a man stood and made his way to the exit. Others began to follow. In dead silence, everyone left the Colosseum.

The year was A.D. 391, and that was the last battle to the death between gladiators in the Roman Colosseum. Never again in the great stadium did men kill each other for the entertainment of the crowd, all because of one tiny voice that could hardly be heard above the crowd. How could he give his life and suffer a senseless death? He had already died before he ever jumped to the floor of the Colosseum. He saw with the eyes of God. He wasn't afraid to tell everyone in the city they were wrong. It happens quite often to people who set their eyes on heaven. Stephen was stoned in Acts 7 because he had died to the world, and he spoke out against evil. John the Baptist didn't win any points with Herod's wife by telling her they shouldn't be married in Mark 6, but his eyes found hope in heaven.

We need a new generation of teens that is willing to look toward heaven instead of the crowds. We need young men and young women who will not go along with the masses. Our world needs to be filled with Christian teens standing up for what they believe in a world that's telling them to sit down and shut up.

We hold a great message of hope out to a world that is filled with hopeless people. An experiment was conducted at the University of North Carolina with two rats. One was put in a jar half-filled with water. A lid was placed on top so it appeared that there was no escape. That rat drowned in three minutes. The other was put in a jar also half-filled, but with a space at the top that was not closed. That rat swam for thirty-six hours before drowning. The difference to the rats was hope, and people are much the same. If we feel there is true hope, we'll keep struggling and fighting.

We can do amazing things if we have hope. Hope keeps the boy who is thinking about suicide from pulling the trigger. Hope keeps the girl from running away from home. Hope keeps the kid from trying drugs, or makes him stop using them once he's seen their worthlessness. Hope says that tomorrow the world will be a better place, and hope is knowing that an Almighty God is on the other side of death.

A student of Friedrich Nietzsche wrote on a school wall, "God is Dead," quoting Mr. Nietzsche.

After Friedrich Nietzsche died another student wrote beside the original quote, "Nietzsche is Dead, signed God." Both the inscriptions stood side by side for students to see. A bush began to grow in front of the original quote. All you could see was, "God is . . . —Nietzsche."

There comes a time when we must consider the course we are setting for our life. We must decide what we will fight for and where we will put our hope. I hope you choose the Eternal and Almighty God.

THOUGHT QUESTIONS FOR CHAPTER 12

1. What are the top five priorities you want to accomplish in life?
2. What suffering have you endured for Christ's cause? If you have not suffered, why do you think Christians do not face persecutions like Paul did?
3. Do you think suicide is caused by suffering or lack of hope?
4. What would you tell someone who was thinking about suicide? What reasons would you use?
5. Would you be willing to die for the cause of Christ?